The Adventures of
the British Citizens

HEATHER YOUNG

For our children, Eleanor and Colin
and our grandchildren Amber and Alfie.

Contents

ACKNOWLEDGEMENTS

This book was written to describe what life was like for Duncan and me, living in El Salvador for four years, and to tell of our experiences there. I would like to thank Nancy Liévano, and Gerardina and Roberto Rosales for coming up with the idea of writing this book and also for their help and encouragement through to completion. Also thanks to Eleanor Young for her assistance in editing, and to Duncan for his help in recalling memories and stories.

1

THE BRITISH ARE COMING!

It was one day in August 2000 when my husband Duncan came home from work and announced that we would be moving to Central America to live and work. At that time he was working as a sewing machine salesman covering Scotland and Ireland; however, it was clear that the clothing manufacturing industry in the UK was in decline and manufacturers were moving their businesses abroad to take advantage of cheaper costs.

Duncan's company instructed their sales staff to establish offices abroad in various countries in order to revitalise the business. Duncan volunteered to go to Central America to investigate the business potential there, and visited Honduras, Guatemala, and El Salvador. After considering all three countries, he established that El Salvador would be the best option, due to the number of American businesses there and their interest in the variety of machinery that he could supply to improve their production costs. So after a few months of preparation, during which we rented out our house, booked flights and said goodbye to our family and friends, everything was in place for us leaving the UK on 20th January, 2001. However, on 13th January, 2001 El Salvador was struck by a 7.7 magnitude earthquake, with nearly one thousand people losing their lives and fifteen hundred people injured. The country was in a state of emergency and the airport was closed. Who could imagine the chaos in this third world country, already suffering with poverty, health issues, and gang activity. Problems with extortion, violent street crimes and also narcotics and guns trafficking being the norm.

As far as we were concerned, the earthquake was quite a blow for us and gave us grave concerns as to how the extra problems it caused might affect our plans. There had to be repercussions but we had no way of knowing exactly what until we arrived in the country. In the meantime we decided to delay our departure for one month to allow the conditions to improve in El Salvador, and so finally left on 13th February, 2001. However, after arriving in Miami to change planes we were shocked to see that all flights to El Salvador had been cancelled due to another earthquake, this time of 6.6 magnitude, exactly one month after the first. Three hundred and fifteen people died and three thousand four hundred people were injured. How terrible for this poor country to suffer once again in such a short time. As far as Duncan and I were concerned, how could we have such terrible luck! Was somebody trying to tell us something? A few days later than planned we finally arrived at Comalapa Airport, El Salvador, complete with thirteen pieces of baggage.

The customs department consisted of a traffic lights conveyor belt system: passengers were invited to push the button, and hopefully gain the green light. However it was no surprise when it turned red for us as this seemed to be the way our luck was going so far. The customs officer looked at us and then looked at our thirteen suitcases and waved us through in disgust! Duncan had arranged accommodation for us in Escalon in the capital city of San Salvador and when we arrived there we were devastated to find that our third floor apartment was now on the first floor; which of course was the result of the earthquakes. It was evident that it was impossible for us to stay there. So here we were, two Scottish people with no knowledge of the country or the language, no friends, and nowhere to go. Thank goodness I had taken my lucky white heather from Scotland with me!

We decided that we would go to the Holiday Inn, Santa Elena, where Duncan had stayed previously. On arriving there, we noticed damage to the building, with brickwork being displaced and large windows being cracked. However, we made this our base for the time being until the estate agent could find another apartment for us. In the meantime the aftershocks were horrendous, but we tried to remain positive and focus on what we were there for – to set up a sewing machine sales business. We decided to advertise for an employee who could speak English to help us find premises as, not speaking Spanish, we found communication difficult. We enquired at the business centre in the hotel about advertising for a staff member and immediately the young receptionist told us that she would like to apply for the position. This is how we found Tanya, whose English was perfect; she even understood us, with our thick Scottish accents!

Tanya started working for us a few weeks later and in no time we secured an office in San Marcos with the help of our lawyer Gustavo, (sourced by Tanya), who was a young, articulate man. Having studied in the States, he had excellent English. Our estate agent had also been in touch, about showing us rental accommodation in Nuevo Cuscatlan. The accommodation was a four-bedroom ground-floor apartment, very spacious and bright and we both loved it immediately. The complex also had a lovely pool, and leisure area, which suited Duncan perfectly. Our lawyer advised Duncan that he would have to sit a test to be able to drive, as his UK licence would not be valid in El Salvador.

So a test was arranged, even though Duncan knew no Spanish. However, the driving examiner didn't seem too interested in Duncan's driving ability, and instead happily pointed out all the places of interest on the route, including the best restaurants. Against all expectations Duncan passed the test, but was then advised that a written test in Spanish had to be taken. This proved to be no problem, though, as the examiner provided Duncan with all the answers (including what lights should be used in fog, which they never have in El Salvador). The rest of the morning was taken up standing in line for blood tests before his licence was granted.

The next item on our list was a car, so off we went to check them out. We eventually decided on a Dodge which was not new but seemed to be in good condition and was big enough and versatile enough to carry machinery. However, knowing nothing about cars and with nobody to advise us (apart from the salesman), we decided that this would be the car for us. Having no knowledge of the roads – and of course satellite navigation had not yet been invented – the only way that we could find our way around was to explore by ourselves. So every Sunday we would take a drive and see where we ended up. We ended up in some scary places, I can tell you, but gradually we gained a basic knowledge of the area.

Driving in El Salvador was not a pleasant experience, with most drivers speeding and driving recklessly. The only way for Duncan to fit in was to drive the same way. The first weekend after moving into the apartment, we decided to visit a Chinese restaurant which was close by. I was worried about going, because of the language barrier, but Duncan was not concerned. He assured me that we would manage. This is where we celebrated our first restaurant meal in El Salvador.

It was a small place and quite busy, but our first problem came when we were presented with the menu, which was of course all in Spanish. Duncan suggested that we order what we normally had in Scotland, which was chicken, and assured me that he could organise that. At this point we were the focus of attention for the whole of the restaurant, mainly because we looked and sounded so different to everybody else, and therefore we were a great source of interest.

The waiter arrived at the table to take our order and I was amazed when Duncan started to (very loudly) do an impression of a chicken, much to the amusement of the waiter and also the assembled audience, who were all in hysterics. I couldn't wait to hear how Duncan was going to do an impression of rice. Just then, another waiter arrived to serve dinner to the next table. Duncan spotted some little bowls of rice and quickly pointed them out to our waiter, saying, "That, that." Again lots of laughter from our audience, who seemed delighted with Duncan's performance and finished off with a round of applause.

Life in El Salvador was certainly going to be interesting. We spent every day preparing the office, for the machines arriving from the UK and Austria. It took a long time to set up the business legally with the appropriate departments and also to apply for our residency. It involved weekly visits to Gustavo's office to sign papers, and numerous trips to the relevant government offices. The red tape was horrendous and sometimes it seemed that no progress was being made at all. However, we had to obey the rules and regulations of the country, and we understood that everything had to be completed to the various departments' satisfaction. In the meantime we advertised by displaying a notice on the office door for a part-time cleaner. The next day there was a long line of people applying for the job. Duncan and Tanya did the interviewing and after seeing lots of applicants they were impressed by a young girl who was really desperate for the job.

Duncan was concerned that she was too young to work and enquired how old she was. Convinced that she was about twelve years old, he was amazed to learn that she was seventeen and had three children. She was offered the job, and she accepted. When she told us her name was Eugenia, Duncan advised her that he could never pronounce that and her new name was Jeannie, and so it was settled, and Jeannie started working a few days later. Eventually all the legalities were completed and we opened for business. The name of the company being Sahl Americas. After only a few weeks in the apartment we received a water bill for six dollars. Suspecting it was for the previous occupant, we decided to pay it anyway and went to the local Bank of Agricola, which was within walking distance. There was a long line (as usual), but eventually it was our turn. We asked if anybody spoke English and by some miracle were taken to a young bank teller who said that she could speak English and would be happy to help us. We presented her with the bill and the six dollars but she told us that there was a problem because we didn't have an account with the bank and therefore we couldn't pay it there. Duncan asked her if he could open an account and produced his passport for identification and fifty dollars. She said this would be fine, and as it would take a few minutes directed us to a waiting area.

The few minutes turned into an hour but eventually we heard a bank teller call out "British Citizen.". This went on a few times and Duncan said that this must have something to do with us as we were the only British people there, and also it was the same teller who had assisted us earlier. Sure enough, it was our teller, who by this time had the attention of the whole bank. She proudly presented Duncan with his bank book in the name of British Citizen! We looked at each other in disbelief. Then we started to laugh and told her that, no, that wasn't his name, as she had taken British Citizen from the heading on the passport and not Duncan Young which was printed inside with all the personal details. At this point she understood and went into fits of uncontrollable laughter. She then proceeded to show all her colleagues the mistake, and they also thought it was hilarious and were laughing and pointing at us. The news quickly spread to the audience in the bank, and they appreciated the joke also. Our faces were scarlet with embarrassment, but half an hour later we left the bank with the book corrected in Duncan's name and the bill paid. We said adios to our new friends, who seemed to be happy that we had provided some welcome entertainment.

2

SPANISH CLASSES

We decided it was time to learn Spanish, and Tanya arranged for us to visit the Escuela Americana International language school in Escalon. We were received by a girl called Lydia who told us that they did not offer Spanish classes at the school, there being no demand for them. However, she could arrange for a teacher to come to our home, and so our first lesson was arranged for the following week. This is how we met Nancy Liévano who was to become our great friend.

Before our first lesson, Nancy called us to get directions to our apartment, and told us later that she could not believe we were speaking English, as our rough Scottish accents made it difficult for her to understand us. I remember thinking that these Spanish lessons were going to be fun.

So gradually we got to know Nancy, and she gave us lessons twice a week. Not just in Spanish, but in history, geography, religious studies and local knowledge. She gave us Spanish homework (which we never did), and was always patient and tried her best to encourage us. We looked forward to our lessons, but did not take them seriously enough, probably because of Nancy's wonderful sense of humour and how she was so interested in hearing our news and of our latest escapades. As a result, class times were taken up having fun, with very little Spanish being spoken by us. I remember one class when Nancy was reading in Spanish and we were supposed to be listening, with questions to be answered later. However, this was at the end of a difficult day in the office and neither of us were in the mood for Spanish. Instead of listening, I was busy colouring in a picture of a boy in my Spanish book, happily selecting red for his hair, and various colours for his striped sweater. Suddenly everything was quiet, the reading having stopped and I jumped when she asked me, what I was doing. Nancy was looking at me in disbelief. Meanwhile Duncan was absorbed trying to fit a sheet of paper through a small gap in the table, and was oblivious to the fact that he was being watched by both of us. Nancy roared with laughter and the Spanish was abandoned for the evening as it was obvious that we were in no mood to concentrate on the lesson.

To be honest, we were hopeless, and all we did was to ruin her English as she learned Scottish words from us. However, she was a great help as she translated all our mail, and advised us generally on life in El Salvador and how to keep safe. She told us never to hail a taxi in the street, not to wear jewellery when we went out, never to go to the bank on the same day each week, and not to eat from the food sellers in the street. All of this advice we were grateful for, but ignored!

3

CATRIONA AND ROBERT

A few weeks after arriving in El Salvador we received a call from Duncan's sister Catriona, asking if she and her husband Robert could come for a visit. We were really excited at this prospect and, because our living-room furniture was quite uncomfortable, decided that this would be the perfect time to replace it.

So we visited a furniture store in Escalon. They had a great selection of furniture in the huge store and we decided on two new sofas, for a great price. The salesman spoke English too, so that made everything so much easier. We paid cash and the delivery was arranged for the following Tuesday, which suited us perfectly. When Duncan arrived home that Tuesday evening, he was disappointed (but not surprised) to find that the sofas had not arrived, and so called the store to find out what the problem was. After conversations with different assistants, he was eventually connected to the salesman who took our order. He explained to Duncan that the furniture could not be delivered because the paperwork had some missing information. Thinking it was our address that had been missed, Duncan offered to give it again, but was astounded to learn that the company could not deliver because they did not know my age. Duncan told the salesman that I was thirty-two (I was actually forty-eight), and the sofas arrived an hour later. To this day we have no idea what that was all about.

Catriona and Robert arrived a few weeks later (complete with snakebite kit!) and we were really excited to welcome them.

El Salvador is a colourful country, with such warm and friendly people and we had a wonderful time, showing Catriona and Robert around and visiting our favourite bars and restaurants. We also visited Mayan ruins at Joya de Ceren, a fascinating archaeological site still being excavated.

We went to Lake Coatepeque, which is a large crater lake, surrounded by woodland hills and very beautiful. Another day we visited Ilobasco, a town in the mountains, which was famous for handmade pottery, we drove there in our car, but halfway there had a puncture. Duncan and Robert managed to change the wheel and we continued our journey. On arriving in the town we spotted a garage and thought this would be an ideal opportunity to get the puncture fixed while we were exploring. We had a great day. Catriona and I visited a little shop and bought some traditional Salvadoran ceramics from a little old lady who looked about a hundred years old. We had lunch outside and, as usual, it wasn't long before we attracted the curiosity of the locals, who must have thought we were aliens, never having seen anything like us before. On returning to the garage, we found that the men had completed the job repairing our wheel and we were so relieved to have it back for our return trip. On leaving the garage, though, a fight started with the workmen. We couldn't understand why, until Robert mentioned that he hoped it was nothing to do with the fifty dollars tip that he had given to the little boy who was with them. Of course it was. You could probably have bought the town for fifty dollars.!

We were sad to see Catriona and Robert leave, but glad that we had been able to show them something of our new adopted, beautiful country and that they survived – and thankfully we never needed the snakebite kit.

Catriona and Robert were to visit us a second time in El Salvador. Once again we were delighted to have them and continue our sightseeing trips and adventures. This time we embarked on a bus trip to Antigua in Guatemala for the weekend. By taking the bus we were able to see a lot of different sites and places on the way. The bus company also provided a packed lunch of tamales, made of dough and filled with meat, cheese and vegetables and which we enjoyed very much. When we reached the Guatemalan border, the bus was stopped by the immigration officers and we were instructed to hand over our passports. This worried us initially, but thankfully they were returned safely to us. While waiting, we attempted to exchange money and also watched people cross the border on foot with many of the women carrying baskets and various other objects on their heads, as was the custom.

After changing buses in Guatemala City we continued our journey and arrived at the Radisson Hotel, in Antigua. Our accommodation was comfortable and in a great location, within walking distance of bars and restaurants in the centre. We also had stunning views of the Acatenango Volcano. In the town centre there was a market selling typical Guatemalan crafts and ceramics and we enjoyed wandering around at our leisure. We met a young girl holding a baby boy, whose name was Anderson. We were intrigued by this but weren't able to establish how his Scottish name came about. Soon we were approached by a young boy who had been hovering around watching us for some time. His English was good (which was fortunate, because our Spanish had not improved much). This boy was extremely skilled in extracting money from us, by joking with us and being generally charming. He followed us around for some time and by the time he left us we were financially much lighter, but very happy to have met him.

We visited several bars and restaurants, enjoying the different experiences and each other's company. On returning to El Salvador, when I casually mentioned to Nancy of our visit, she was horrified. She explained that this trip was extremely dangerous, as the buses were regularly held up on that route by bandits and many kidnappings and fatalities resulted. She was horrified further when she heard about the tamales that we ate (and enjoyed) while on the bus. She said "Didn't I tell you never to eat food prepared and sold from people in the street, because of their lack of hygiene methods and facilities?" It was true that some people prepared food in their portable bath-tubs and had no running water, and this would probably be the same food we ate on the bus. She also reminded us that we were extremely lucky not to have been stopped as being Europeans: we would have been prime candidates for kidnap-ping, I reminded her of my non-existent cooking skills and how Duncan advised me if I ever did get kidnapped, just to cook for my captors and they would soon release me!

4

NANCY FARLOW

One Sunday afternoon while having lunch in La Hola Beto's, in the Zona Rosa area, we watched as two men crossed the street to enter the restaurant. We knew immediately that they were not locals because they looked European and were laden with lots of souvenirs – mainly Salvadoran dolls and pottery – and so obviously had been tourist shopping. This was Vinnie and Brian, two English men who were engineers, working in El Salvador for a few months. They sat at the next table to us and we were happy to see them and had lots to talk about. They suggested that we visit the

British Club in Escalon and, never having heard of it, we were keen to go.

The club was full of information about the UK, with books and magazines in English available for borrowing, a picture of the Queen on the wall, and lots of news about the UK displayed. However, we were the only British people there and we were not received warmly. I thought: how typically British. In fact it was as though they resented us for being British. We did find out, though, that the British Ambassador was from Scotland and so there was another link. Patrick Morgan was from Greenock, and was happy to talk to me when I called him one day, to advise him of our residency and business enterprise. He was extremely friendly and encouraging and although we intended to meet up with him, sadly we never did.

One day, Vinnie and Brian took us to a different bar, owned by a Canadian lady called Nancy Farlow. It was a new bar, built in the Santa Elena area, close to the huge American Embassy. Nancy thought that by opening her bar in this location she would have lots of American customers. She was delighted to see us, and became a valuable friend. She gave us lots of good advice and we enjoyed her company, visiting with our friends to eat and promoting her business whenever we could.

Before we left the UK, a friend informed us that a local bookshop was raising funds for El Salvador. She gave us the contact details of the priest responsible for this and suggested that we contact him. He was anxious to meet us before we left Scotland as he had a friend, who was also a priest, living and working in El Salvador, and wanted us to pass on some books to him. So a few weeks after arriving in El Salvador we contacted Father Tim and arranged to meet in the El Bodegon restaurant in Escalon. Duncan and I were quite nervous to meet him (not being Catholic), so we persuaded Nancy Liévano to accompany us (as she was Catholic), thinking it would bridge the gap, which it did, as conversation flowed easily and Nancy was delighted with Tim's knowledge of Spanish.

Father Tim had lived in Soyapango for twelve years and was involved in working with the local gangs. His work was very dangerous, and he had shocking stories to tell. He was trying to rehabilitate the young men in the gangs and had some degree of success, but also many failures. One particular time he had taken some gang members to the beach on a day out, as they had never seen the ocean before, but it ended tragically, when a waiter died during a disagreement with the gang members. There were lots of similar stories and it was obvious life was not easy for him. He was planning to go to Chicago to study psychology, in order to be better equipped to deal with the situation in El Salvador. It was a really interesting evening and he mentioned there was a Scottish nun living in the country also, and a Scottish bar there too. He offered to take us to the bar and so we went, happy to hear of another Scottish connection. The bar of course was Scottish themed and had huge pictures of Mel Gibson as Braveheart on the walls. We only visited it a few times as it was far from our apartment and not in a particularly safe area. However, we never did meet the Scottish nun, probably because we would not have had much in common with her!

5

JESSICA, ROBERT AND EDDIE

Our Spanish lessons continued and we looked forward to Nancy's visits and updating her with our news and enjoying her company. Not much Spanish was being spoken, though, because we were too busy talking to her in English about our adventures. One day Nancy arrived for our Spanish class and was surprised to find that Duncan had gone to Mexico on business, leaving me alone. He had assured me that I would be fine, and just to make sure that the apartment was secure. I have to admit that I was quite nervous being by myself as we'd only been in El Salvador a few months, and did not know many people. Nancy, however, was so kind and considerate and on hearing that I was alone, and had never been out since Duncan left, suggested we go to Mr Donut's cafe instead of having our usual lesson. This was the beginning of our friendship. One day she invited me to a special presentation for her mother, who was involved in a women's association and was being presented with the Woman of the Year award. This is where I met Nancy's mother Cony and also her sister Ana Maria. It was a fabulous evening, with lots of compliments given to Cony, who was a worthy candidate for this award. The evening ended with everybody singing the national anthem of El Salvador, which I loved because it was so tuneful and unforgettable. (It is called Saludemos La Patria Orgullosos)

We met Nancy's daughter, Jessica, when she was eleven. She would translate for me when we went out together and would stay at our apartment when Duncan was away on business. She was great company for me. Another day Nancy and I went to pick up her nephews from the International School. This was the first time that I met Robert, who was seventeen, and Eddie who was sixteen. They were great fun and joined us often for our Spanish classes. Sometimes we would go to Nancy's Bar to eat; and other times we would order pizza to eat at home. One particular night Duncan insisted on ordering the pizza to be delivered. He dialled the number and confidently gave the order in Spanish, requesting one half of the pizza to be with vegetables and the other pepperoni. I was impressed. He gave his name and address to the lady but then he called to me that the lady said there was a problem with the order. She said, "Mi Casa en Soyapango." It was because he had made a mistake dialling the number and called a private house instead of Dominos. It was hilarious, and he had to call Dominos and go through it all again.

6

THE ORPHANAGE

The setting up of the business was slow but eventually completed and we were ready for the machinery when it arrived from the UK and Austria. A colleague of Duncan's was there to help him set up and display the machines in the office, so that customers could see them in operation. Tanya, of course, would translate for Duncan, which was a great help. I remember Duncan instructing her on sales technique, especially on the automated machine which was really impressive and required the operator to have little skill. He told her amongst other things to inform the customer that this machine doesn't get sick, doesn't take time off and doesn't get pregnant! Tanya couldn't do this without laughing.

Soon we were busy, either with Duncan and Tanya visiting factories or with customers coming to the office. Our social life improved too. One day while in a superstore we were approached by an American gentleman who invited us to the Union Church, which was for all Christian denominations. We were given a lovely welcome by the congregation, who were really friendly and excited to see us. I started a conversation with an American lady holding a baby. She told me that she rescued the baby from an orphanage when he was really sick. By some miracle, he survived and, because of the fear that his health would deteriorate if he returned to the orphanage, she was allowed to keep him. However, she was moving to Honduras soon and so had to leave the baby. She asked if I was interested in having him but I had to decline. She then invited me to visit the orphanage with her and I accepted.

Since Catriona and Robert were due to arrive in the next few days, I arranged for Catriona and I to go together with her. It was an experience that I'll never forget. The small building had been badly damaged by the earthquakes and half of the roof was missing. It was very dark inside, with approximately forty kids running around, and one little dog. They were all looked after by Tia Ana, who did her best with this impossible task. The kids ranged from babies only a few months old up to teenagers, who helped to look after the younger ones. The kids were about to have lunch of rice and beans and took their seats at the table. Tia Ana prayed the Grace and the kids looked so cute, with praying hands and closed eyes, thanking the Lord for what he had provided. It was such an emotional experience for me and I decided I had to support this orphanage by buying food and medicines, and so this was the start of my monthly visits. Catriona and Robert helped financially also and even supported a teenager called Douglas by paying for his education – books and school expenses. My monthly trips to the orphanage continued until we left El Salvador.

Some of the congregation at the Union Church were hoping to open a new orphanage. After much planning and organisation, premises were found and altered to suit the children's needs. Nancy Hoffman was involved in this valuable project and when the day came for the children to be moved in, (with Tia Ana), she invited me to help out. It was extremely well organised, and the children were all given a shower, on arrival, and also new clothes. Then they were shown their new accommodation. This orphanage still exists today, and is called 'La Casa de mi Padre,' (My Father's House). It has progressed immensely since that first day, and countless children have benefited from the education and safe haven it provides.

7

UNION CHURCH

We settled into life easily in El Salvador, which was amazing given the fact that everything was so different to what we were used to – the language, weather, food, and the culture. We found our circle of friends growing fast too, which was mainly due to the Union Church that we attended. The congregation consisted of different Christian denominations. Protestant, Catholic, Baptist, Lutheran, to name a few. Pastor Jeff therefore had a difficult job of keeping everybody happy spiritually, and adjustments were made to prayers and services, to avoid conflict of beliefs.

Of course we were the only Scottish people attending and to begin with were a great source of interest to the congregation. Many Americans attended and soon we had lots of invitations for dinner, which we gratefully accepted, as I was no Martha Stewart. The inside walls of the church were decorated with flags of the different nations attending and Pastor Jeff asked us to provide a Scottish flag. We gave him the Lion Rampant which in our opinion was more colourful that the Scottish Saltire flag and we admired it as it hung proudly on the wall with its companions. However, when Catriona visited and attended the church with us, she was surprised to see the flag, and soon pointed out that we fly the Lion Rampant, mainly when we go to war, so therefore this was maybe not appropriate for a church. She advised that the Saltire flag would be more suitable, but we decided to keep quiet, as the damage was done and we were too embarrassed to correct it! I wonder if it's still hanging there today?

8

NANCY HOFFMAN

In church one Sunday the pastor introduced an American lady who was sitting in front of us. He explained that she requested to address the church, to relate to the congregation, a recent frightening experience. This was Nancy Hoffman. She told the congregation that she and her friend Nora, were recently visiting a beach house and, as they waited for the security gates to be opened, were approached by two men with guns, demanding money. Nora, very bravely, instructed the men to leave immediately and not to hurt them, as both ladies had no cash with them. To her astonishment the men turned and ran off. Both ladies were extremely shaken by the experience and it was reported to the police.

Eventually the men were caught and Nora attended the court for the sentencing. She asked to speak to the judge and pleaded for mercy for the men, explaining that nobody had been injured and hoped that this experience would, with the help of God, change their attitudes, and lives.. The judge relented and they did indeed receive a reduced sentence, and hopefully a positive change in their lives resulted. Hearing that story, impressed us that morning and resulted in a wonderful friendship with Nancy Hoffman. It reminded us also that this was just one example of how dangerous this country could be, especially for foreigners like ourselves. However, it did not take away the love that we had for El Salvador and the people, and we understood that poverty and hopelessness play a large part in causing people to do desperate things in order to survive.

9

EXHIBITION

We discovered that there was going to be a clothing machine exhibition at La Feria in San Salvador, and Duncan thought this would be an excellent opportunity to reach new customers and also demonstrate his machines.

It took a lot of organisation and hard work for us to be ready for this and Tanya was a great help making the arrangements. However, she pointed out that since we couldn't speak Spanish and we were expecting a lot of customers, it would be a good idea to get another Spanish-speaking demonstrator to help out.

After discussing this with Nancy Liévano and gaining her permission, it was agreed that we would invite her nephew Robert, aged seventeen, to join us for the exhibition, as he spoke Spanish fluently. Robert was delighted to be able to assist us and helped with the construction of the machines. Duncan gave him a short tutorial on the machines and their capabilities, so he could explain this to potential customers.

On the first day of the exhibition, lots of people attended and we were all extremely busy on the stand. None of our competitors had similar machines, so we had a lot of interest and questions from interested customers, especially for the Austrian automatic machine, which was amazing. Robert watched Duncan carefully explain to customers in English how the machine processed the fabric and at the end a tee-shirt was produced. This happened with very little interaction from the operator and therefore minimal training was required. Robert soon mastered this demonstration efficiently and the next day was ready to progress to a different type of machine.

After his tutorial from Duncan, he was ready to demonstrate a machine that inserted wires into bras. Duncan had carefully explained to him that this machine was especially valuable to manufacturers, as many had experienced problems with the sharp underwires escaping from the stitching and protruding through the fabric, injuring the wearers. Indeed, a few clothing manufacturers had been sued in court for damages. Duncan, being Duncan, as usual found it best to mime what happened when the wires lost their place, leaving the bra cups flopping and the breasts unsupported. Robert took all this information seriously and when it was his turn to explain the workings of the machine, he performed perfectly, complete with the flopping demonstration as instructed by Duncan. In the meantime, I was worried about explaining this to Nancy and the only thing I could think of to tell her was that she gave us a boy, but we sent back a man!

10

CHANGES

Business was improving steadily, and the sale of sewing machine parts especially was proving to be popular. This gave Duncan access to companies and soon his reputation for solving production and engineering problems spread within the clothing industry. Machinery was installed on trial in companies, giving managers the opportunity to assess them in operation before committing to buying. So overall the business was building up nicely, or so we thought.

Suddenly we were hit by two major problems. The first was that Tanya informed us she would require some leave of absence, as she was pregnant. This was a big shock to us as we realised she would need time off, before and after the birth, and how would we cope without her? However, she came up with a solution. Her brother had recently returned to El Salvador after living in the States, and could replace her until she was ready to resume work. After meeting José we readily agreed, as he was friendly and likeable. He proved to be a valuable asset to the company, was extremely interested in the sewing machine business and keen that we should do well.

The second problem was that we received notice from our landlord requesting that we vacate the apartment, as it was required for a relative. This could not have happened at a worse time as we were preparing to return to the UK for our first holiday, just before Christmas. Again, José was eager to help and soon found us a lovely apartment in a gated community in Escalon, and close to Nancy Liévano and her family. We were happy and especially as he had negotiated a much cheaper rent also, and so we arranged to move into the apartment after our return from the UK.

11

EARTHQUAKE

One beautiful day while sunbathing by the pool at our apartment, we were puzzled when everything went deathly quiet. The birds stopped chirping and the sky turned a strange colour. Then all of a sudden the birds began squawking and dogs barking, and it was clear that they sensed something. This was followed by a rumbling sound and the earth started shaking. It was another earthquake! The water in the pool was moving from side to side and ended up pouring over the sides onto the grass. Although it didn't last for long it was a terrifying experience. However, thankfully, the only damage to our apartment was to our entry door – it had dropped on one side, making it difficult to open – but it could have been so much worse.

This was just one danger that had to be endured in El Salvador. Another was the weather. There are only two seasons; the rainy season, which begins in May and lasts for six months, and then the dry season following. Being a tropical country, the average temperature is 74 degrees Fahrenheit (23 degrees Centigrade). When it rained it was torrential, with roads being turned into rivers, making driving impossible. The force of the water removed drain covers, leaving manholes uncovered and causing many accidents.

For us the main problem caused in the rainy season was the flooding of our apartment, as we were on the ground floor. The drains would be unable to cope with the volume of water and become blocked, causing the water to flood the hallway up to our apartment door. On one occasion when this happened, Duncan went to investigate the problem. He met a man in the grounds of the apartment block, who was obviously concerned at the rising level of the water too. Duncan started the conversation using his usual mode of mimicking, by placing his hands round his own throat and making a choking sound, to indicate that the drains were obstructed. The man looked at him in astonishment (obviously perplexed by Duncan's actions) and replied, "Yes, buddy, the drains are blocked," in perfect English. Of course, Duncan had assumed that his companion spoke no English and so, face red with embarrassment, beat a hasty retreat.

12

THE CAR

After taking delivery of the Dodge, which seemed perfect both for our leisure and business needs, there was no holding us back. We visited numerous places in El Salvador, and surprisingly found our way around quite easily to government offices, banks and post offices., even without satellite navigation to help us. After some time, however, the car started to present problems. One day, Duncan and Tanya were visiting a customer in Apopa, which is twenty-six miles from San Marcos, leaving me in charge of the office. After a few hours, of no communication from them and being unable to contact them, I started to worry about their safety. Eventually, Tanya called to say that the car had broken down, (and as she described it), "In a place that God forgot")! It was only due to the goodness of some men passing in a truck, who had helped to get them to a garage in Apopa, that the car was repaired. Of course, the mobile phone signal there was non-existent, which was the reason for no contact.

Another day Duncan called to say he was outside Mr Donuts in Antigua, Cuscatalan, close to our apartment. Thinking he was calling to take my order, I proceeded to give him my list of the delicious goodies – two chocolate, two caramel, two coconut towers – before he interrupted me by shouting that he was not calling about Mr Donuts, but to tell me that the car was stuck outside it!

On another occasion Duncan was travelling thirty-four miles to Santa Ana to visit a customer when the car broke down. Amazingly, once again a group of men stopped and helped him to push the car to a local garage where it was repaired. Duncan repaid their help by taking them all for lunch. When I asked how he managed with the language barrier, he said that it was fine, and that I worried too much about small things like that!

The car was taken to a repair garage in Santa Elena numerous times, resulting in us being known to all the staff there. The manager insisted on calling Duncan, Señor Stewart and would contact us at the office, each time the car was ready to be collected, asking for Señora Young and Señor Stewart, which left Tanya puzzled. We could only assume that he had seen Duncan's full name on a document and had been confused with his middle name. But it was evident that we could not continue with the car failing and causing us to be in dangerous situations. Also, the costs of the repairs were enormous: we had replaced most of the engine by this time. We decided, therefore, that it was time for a new car. It was a big relief when we took delivery of a brand new Isuzu truck, and one less problem for us to deal with. Duncan was able to travel safely in a reliable car and continue with the joys of driving around El Salvador!

13

SUPERMARKET

Each week we would go food shopping in the Superselectos Supermarket, close to our apartment. On one occasion I wanted to buy some cold ham and since I knew that none of the assistants spoke English, I rehearsed carefully in my mind how to say this in Spanish. So as per my Spanish teacher, Nancy's instructions, I asked nervously, "Media libra de jamon por favor." The assistant smiled and proceeded to cut the half a pound of ham, leaving me looking on happily, relieved that she understood my Spanish–Scottish request. Duncan in the meantime had been busy selecting the vegetables that we would need for the week, and on returning was amazed to see a huge pyramid of ham on the scales and the assistant still adding more. He laughed and asked me, "I wonder who's buying all that ham?"

To which I replied, "Me!"

Duncan said, "Why are you buying so much?"

I replied, "I think she misunderstood the quantity that I asked for."

Meanwhile the girl was still happily cutting. Duncan said in a panic, "Then tell her to stop!"

I said nervously "I'm trying to think of the Spanish for that!"

Duncan, unable to contain himself any longer, shouted, "Senorita, WHOA!" also demonstrating a cutting movement with his hands. The assistant understood perfectly and stopped cutting. What a relief! We left the supermarket with our enormous package of ham, which lasted us for several weeks, and I remember thinking: must pay more attention in our Spanish classes!

On another occasion and unfortunately in the same supermarket, I suffered a second embarrassing experience. This time I wanted to buy cigars for my dad, and not wanting a repeat performance of the last time, I asked Nancy to give me the exact phrase in Spanish. She advised me to say, "Tienes habanos por favor?" Which I did very slowly and carefully to the assistant, who replied "Si." She gestured for me to follow her and I did. Right to the back of the store, through a passage and up a stairway. I was thinking by this time, there's something not right here, but unable to stop her, I carried on. Until we came to the bathrooms, which she proudly displayed to me in all their glory.

I told her, "Necesita habanos." (I need cigars)

She replied, smiling, "Si los banos." (Yes, the bathrooms). Confusing my Spanish for cigars with bathrooms, she must have been thinking by this time I was desperate to use the bathrooms. So she gently pushed me in and closed the door. I had no option but to comply and when I exited found her patiently waiting to lead me back. Once again I left that store with a red face and a feeling of not quite sure of what had just happened. Life in El Salvador was certainly not boring!

14

WALLACE

There were a few things that we found difficult to get used to in El Salvador. One was, the insects and cockroaches were everywhere. The other was that we had a particular problem in the apartment during the rainy season when the drains would block. Being on the ground floor, the water would flood the apartment, which was bad enough, but this would cause the cockroaches to climb up above the water level to escape, and resulting in a disgusting line of them on the walls. It was horrific and it took lots of complaints to our landlord before it was fixed., by the maintenance department, who eventually made the appropriate pipe repairs.

Nancy Liévano advised us always to wear something on our feet indoors as there was a danger of tiny insects crawling inside any cuts that we might have and therefore cause an infection. Information like this was useful because we would never have experienced anything like this in the UK, and therefore were not aware of any danger. We decided to get a cat, in the hope that it would eliminate insects and cockroaches. Tanya suggested a pet shop that she knew and offered to take me there. When we arrived, we saw two tiny Siamese kittens sitting sadly in the window. The decision of which one to get was decided for me because somebody was already purchasing one, leaving the other one for me. The assistant put my kitten in a cardboard box and taped on the lid with a few air holes on top. When we got back to the car I immediately removed the lid because the kitten was frantically trying to escape. It was the tiniest, skinniest kitten we had ever seen and we loved him immediately. Duncan decided that he should be called Wallace, after William Wallace, the Scottish hero. He settled in quickly and cleared the apartment of all the cockroaches by flipping them on their backs, and using them as footballs around the apartment. Every morning, we would collect the dead footballs and dispose of them. Wallace was indeed a hero! Unfortunately after two years, Wallace suddenly went missing and despite searching tirelessly for him we never found him.

15

HOME VISIT

We returned home to Scotland for Christmas and were very excited to see our family. Our son, Colin was still living in Perth and our daughter, Eleanor was coming from her home in Hednesford. We were desperate to see them after nearly a year, and happy that we would all be together again. On arriving at Edinburgh airport, there was a great welcome for us with my parents Grace and Allan, my auntie and uncle, May and Tom, and also, Catriona and Robert. It was weird getting used to the different weather again but we were so delighted to be back that we hardly noticed the rain and snow. We were also able to check on our house, which was currently being occupied by tenants from Kuwait and their five children.

The time passed quickly, though, and soon it was time to return to El Salvador. We were distraught at having to leave our friends and family, but were committed to our new life and business and therefore had no choice. It was, however, a comfort to know that the situation was temporary, as we expected to be there for only another year.

On returning to El Salvador, it was great to see Nancy Liévano and her family again, and we were able to meet her son Frank, aged fifteen, who was currently on holiday from Burbank, California. After a few uneasy weeks we settled back into the lifestyle again, enjoying the weather and the fellowship of our church and friends. Our new apartment too was lovely, and came with Laura, a maid. Which to begin with, we found quite awkward, but we soon got used to her twice weekly visits, and soon she was indispensable to us. The apartment was on two levels, with a sitting room and bedroom downstairs and kitchen, dining room and two bedrooms upstairs. No pool, but it had a lovely garden which was tended for us by a gardener. We particularly liked the area, with the Superselectos Supermarket being close by for our food shopping, together with a number of restaurants and bars which we could explore. The area was safe, too, which was a comfort and Francisco Flores lived around the corner from us. Therefore, if it was good enough for the President of El Salvador, then it was good enough for us!

16

SARAH-JAYNE AND COLIN

We were excited to hear that Colin was coming to visit us with his partner Sarah-Jayne. They arrived with clothes and toys gifted by friends and relatives in Scotland to donate to the orphanage. We were grateful for everything, and a visit was arranged so they could see for themselves the horrific conditions that these children were living in, and be able to tell everyone in Scotland that their kindness was appreciated and desperately needed.

Tanya took us to the supermarket to buy the usual supplies, and Sarah-Jayne and Colin provided extra sweets and juices, as special treats for the children. As usual the building was in darkness when we arrived. Soon the door was answered and we were given a great welcome by excited kids and the light was switched on for us. Sarah-Jayne and Colin were shocked at the condition of the run-down building and the lack of essential items required to care for forty children. There were only a few small chairs and tables and none of the home comforts we are used to. When we produced the toys, colouring books and pencils, the children formed an orderly line to receive their gifts. Some of the bigger children helped to look after the smaller ones. Sarah-Jayne asked a girl carrying a small baby if she could hold the baby and reluctantly she agreed. However, the girl watched over the baby constantly, making sure that she was safe and wasn't taken away. Although our visit was not a pleasant experience, it was worthwhile because Tia Ana and the children were delighted to see us and also desperate for the much-needed supplies.

Sarah-Jayne and Colin took the chance to experience as much as they could of El Salvador. They were happy to explore shops, bars and nightclubs by themselves, and of course we did our best to make sure that they were safe. However, they did not seem to be intimidated by the dangers. On visiting The Jungle nightclub in Zona Rosa, they were fascinated to see a long line of men waiting, not to collect their jackets at the end of the evening, (which happens in the UK), but to collect their guns. They also discovered, when a disagreement occurred between two men, that it was their bodyguards that participated in the fight, on their bosses behalf.

On one occasion the four of us went out for the day. Duncan was driving our car and on discovering that he had taken the wrong road, quickly did a U-turn. Unfortunately, the police spotted him. They stopped us and indicated that he should get out of the car. Of course they had no English, and we had no Spanish, so it was impossible to communicate. I tried to call Tanya, but as there was no reply, I called Nancy Farlow at her bar for advice. In the meantime, however, the situation between Duncan and the policemen had deteriorated (probably because Duncan was shouting at them). Colin advised me to tell Duncan to calm down because the policemen had guns and did not look amused. After reminding Duncan that he was dealing with armed policemen, he quickly quietened, and I was able to explain the situation on the phone to Nancy. She told me to pass the phone to the policeman and she would deal with it. A minute later the policeman, in fits of laughter, handed back the phone and indicated that we could go. Still laughing and shaking his head, he was explaining the conversation to his colleague, who was also laughing. We did not hang around though to get an explanation and nervously resumed our journey. The next day we visited Nancy's Bar. We asked her how she resolved the situation with the policemen and she told us that it was really simple. She explained to them that we had recently moved here to open a business, and that we were not bad people because we had helped a lot of locals in various ways. However, we were a bit dumb, and got ourselves into crazy situations. She also invited them to come and have dinner and drinks at her bar and they happily accepted. Problem solved!

17

THE UNIVERSITY

One day after church we were approached by an American friend who asked us to come to the university where he lectured, to address his class and recite some poetry. Don taught literature and his students were currently studying the work of the Scottish poet Robert Burns. He thought it would be interesting for them to hear the poems in a Scottish accent, and so it was arranged for us to visit a few days later. I downloaded and printed off some information for the class and after a few performance rehearsals, we were ready to address them at the Universidad Tecnologica.

There were approximately thirty students in the class and after being introduced, Duncan began by giving a brief history of the life of Robert Burns. We then each recited a poem, followed by a discussion on the work of Burns and his life. Lastly we invited questions from the class on anything to do with Burns, Scotland and the United Kingdom. We found the students to be extremely interested in both the poetry and us. They asked many questions about life in Scotland – its climate, the political situation, Margaret Thatcher, and also the Scottish national dress. Duncan explained in detail the history of the clans, the kilt, and so on, and waited for the question that everybody asked: was it true that nothing was worn under the kilt? Much hilarity followed when Duncan confirmed this to be correct, and when a student asked why this was so, Duncan replied, "Because if you wear something under the kilt, then it becomes a skirt!" He then recited the speech from Braveheart (in the style of Mel Gibson), and finishing with the Freedom salute! Resulting in cheering from the students.

We finished off by singing Auld Lang Syne, which was written by Robert Burns and is known around the world. The class sang it back to us in Spanish, and it concluded a delightful evening. We repeated the lesson twice more for different classes and were presented with a gift of lovely mugs from the university, which we still have today.

18

ADRIANA

Tanya returned to work after her maternity leave and the birth of a baby girl, and José went back to the states. However, it was evident quite quickly that Tanya's family responsibilities were taking up all of her time and energy, and that she could no longer commit to the full time position that we offered. Reluctantly, therefore we decided to let her go. We were extremely fond of Tanya and this was a decision that was not taken lightly. However, we had no choice as the UK office was impatient for sales and the business had to take priority. Our lawyers Ana Maria and Miguel Sol, came to our rescue and offered to help us to find a new secretary. Interviews were arranged at their law firm offices and the position was offered, by a unanimous decision, to an extremely capable girl called Adriana Aguilar. She had been educated at the fee-paying British School in El Salvador (Academia Britanica Cuscatleca), and so was familiar with our British ways and customs and of course spoke excellent English.

We were lucky to have her and Adriana was to become a great friend to us, and was always reliable and hardworking. One of the things we loved about her was her sense of humour and we had many hilarious experiences on a day-to-day basis, in the office and on our visits to banks, factories and government offices. On one occasion Duncan suggested that Adriana ask some local men to help him to unload a huge container filled with sewing machines. Since there were always unemployed men hanging around the streets, looking for work, we didn't expect there to be a problem. However, after about twenty minutes, Adriana returned accompanied by a bare chested 'gentleman' covered in tattoos. We knew immediately that this individual was a member of a gang, and by the look on Adriana's face, she knew also. A conversation took place with Adriana translating, and we discovered he was a member of the Maras Dieciocho, who were extremely violent and dangerous. I was sure that we were going to die that day! Meanwhile Duncan instructed Adriana to tell him that we needed several men to help him unload the container and firmly laid down the terms and conditions of the job, which included money, food and beer! I remember thinking, is he nuts? This guy could cut our heads off and not give us a second thought, and Duncan's the one giving HIM orders! Amazingly though, he agreed and six similar men turned up for work the next day. We were really nervous all day having them on our premises, but they worked tirelessly and completed the job earlier than expected. Duncan was delighted with his new friends and this was to be the start of several collaborations with them, in which they treated us with mutual respect.

19

BUSINESS EXPERIENCES

We were having mixed success with the business. Machine sales were not as good as we expected. We decided it would be a good idea to rent machines to customers, especially when companies were unable to buy due to cash flow problems. This gave us a reasonable income and bought us some extra time until sales increased. What was the point of having a large stock of machines in the office when they could be earning us rental fees? The sewing machine parts sales were proving to be successful too. So all in all we were doing fine. Unfortunately, though, our collaboration with our lawyer Gustavo, was coming to an end. Although his help had been invaluable in setting up the business, it was impossible to deal with him now as he had become more successful and was busy with his increasing client base. Therefore, after discussing with Nancy Liévano, we decided to request that her sister and brother in law, Ana Maria and Miguel Sol, act as our legal representatives.

They proved to be a great help by advising us about the business and the legal requirements of the country. On one occasion, when a customer repeatedly refused to pay outstanding machine rental fees, we had no option but to request that they be returned. We were astounded when the customer refused and therefore had no option but to seek Ana Maria and Miguel's advice. They readily took on the challenge by contacting the customer and offering different payment options, but with no success. Ana Maria suggested that we hire security staff to turn up at the company unannounced to seize the machines. This was the last resort as we had tried everything to reach an amicable agreement with this company. We all agreed that this was the only option left to us. Plans were made for the operation, vans were rented, and armed security men were hired, with Ana Maria taking charge of everything. On the day, everything went smoothly, with the security guards doing their job, and the machines being quickly loaded onto the transportation with no opposition from the factory management. Ana Maria did suffer some verbal intimidating threats, but thankfully nothing came of it. We were relieved when this frightening experience was over, and one that we did not want to repeat.

One day Duncan received a request from a factory run by the army in El Salvador, expressing interest in buying machinery. The army personnel managed the factory in production of tee-shirts and other clothing for the army recruits. They were especially interested in the automatic hemming machine. This machine was made in Austria, designed to produce hems automatically while requiring no skill from the operator. It was extremely efficient and fast. The army personnel visited our office to see the machine in operation and were impressed with the results. They intended to produce tee-shirts required by the army in action in the Iraq War. They invited us to place a tender with the government for the funding. This was quite a complicated procedure but Adriana took charge and soon all the paperwork was completed to the government's strict rules. We were disappointed to learn that we had competition from other companies, but were confident that none could provide the technology and training that we offered. Just to complicate matters further, the date for the tender was in December when we would be in the UK for Christmas. However, Adriana once more assured us that she would manage everything. We were delighted when she called to inform us that our tender had been successful and the order for the machine had been placed by the government! Also further machine orders were being considered. This was an important milestone for us and enabled the business to continue in El Salvador for the foreseeable future.

20

NANCY LIÉVANO

We continued with our Spanish lessons, seeing Nancy at least twice weekly. We also met her sister Gerardina and brother-in-law Roberto, the parents of Robert and Eddie. They were extremely warm and friendly and we were delighted to receive an invitation to Robert's graduation in the Presidente Hotel, in San Salvador. It was a lovely evening, and Duncan and I were joined at our table by delightful people who made us really welcome, despite our lack of Spanish. One elderly lady was extremely interested in us and it was not long before she asked the same old question about our national dress. What did men wear under the kilt? She went into fits of laughter when we told her "Nada", (nothing), and she excitedly passed the information to all our table companions, who also found it to be hilarious. This revelation broke the ice and resulted in a fabulous evening with our new friends.

We also had regular contact with Nancy's mother Cony, sister Ana Maria and brother-in-law Miguel (who were now our lawyers). They had two cute children, Gracielita and Miguelito. Another family member was Nancy's aunt Tia Ity. So we had a whole family in El Salvador who befriended us and gave us comfort while we were so far away from our own family in the UK. However, things were about change when Nancy suddenly told us that she was moving back to Los Angeles with Jessica, Robert and Eddie. They were all anxious to return and, although sad to leave their family, they recognised that they would have a better life in California. With the prospect of more opportunities and also they were excited to be reunited with Frank, Geri and Roberto.

This was devastating news for us as we had come to rely on Nancy a lot for advice and knowledge and most importantly for her friendship. The business brought us many problems and it was helpful to discuss these with Nancy and hear her point of view and also be guided by advice from a Salvadoran perspective. It was a sad day for us when she left, but we promised to keep in touch and hoped that a visit could be arranged sometime to Los Angeles. Indeed, over thirty trips have taken place since then to Los Angeles, from not just Scotland, but also from China, Thailand and Mexico, by both Duncan and myself individually and together. We always have a fabulous time, catching up with our Salvadoran family and enjoying our special friendship!

21

THE CHURCHILL BAR

There are a number of beautiful hotels in San Salvador. One of our favourites was the Princess Hotel, which housed the Churchill Bar. The decor was very impressive, with stunning woodwork panelling on the walls, and artwork of Winston Churchill. It was also extremely comfortable, with elegant leather sofas, and we looked forward to our visits there very much. Even better, it had a two-for-one happy hour every Monday night. Therefore, this is where we could be found between six and seven every Monday, together with Nancy Farlow (from the bar), and another friend Wende.

On one particular happy hour night, we parked the car, as usual, outside the school, just across from the hotel. On returning to the car I remarked to Duncan that I saw somebody in the car and immediately thought that I was looking at the wrong car. Duncan replied that it was our car and somebody was stealing it! He immediately took off at speed to challenge the intruder and began shouting. At the same time the armed guard outside the school realised what was happening and began shooting. This horrified me and I called to the guard to stop. In the meantime, though, Duncan was calling out, "Kill him!" Thankfully the guard missed and the intruder took off with Duncan in hot pursuit, jumping hedges and walls to try to catch him. However, it was impossible as the would-be thief was young and fit and also had local knowledge of the area.

Duncan gave up and returned to the car to assess the damage. There was a broken window and items strewn over the car but nothing of any value was missing. Only an umbrella and notebook which the intruder had thrown at Duncan during the chase. I remarked to Duncan that I couldn't believe he was encouraging the guard to shoot the thief, as the crime was not worth taking a life for, but he disagreed, saying that shooting was too good for the intruder! We continued our journey home, a little shaken but unhurt, and it didn't deter us from meeting our friends there the next week!

22

SAD EXPERIENCES

One morning Adriana and I were driving to an appointment at Ana Maria and Miguel's office to sign some papers, when we saw a shocking sight. Walking down the road in full view of everyone was a young girl, approximately eighteen or nineteen years old, completely naked. I couldn't believe my eyes and I knew that we had to do something to help this poor girl. Luckily there was a Superselectos Supermarket close by and so we stopped and bought some clothes and sandals for her. It took us only a few minutes searching before we found her again in a little area where local women were cooking and serving pupusas (cheese tortillas), to customers, who didn't seem to be bothered by the young girl sitting on the ground at their feet. Adriana instructed me to stay in the car while she gave the girl the clothes. It appeared that the girl was mentally handicapped but she did as Adriana instructed and put the clothes on. It was one of the most disturbing sights I have ever seen, and one that I could not ignore.

On another occasion an old man appeared in our office. He was obviously homeless because his clothes were worn and dirty. He told us that he wasn't feeling well and was looking for medication for a headache and could we help. I produced paracetamol pills and Adriana instructed him on the dosage, (hoping he was paying attention and wouldn't overdose), and told him to come back the next day, just so that we could check on him. He was such a jolly soul and had a permanent smile on his face despite his desperate situation. As he turned to leave, I noticed that his shirt at the back was completely non-existent because his bare skin was exposed for the world to see, Amazingly, though, it was intact at the front, and I could just imagine him getting dressed that morning, putting his shirt on and being happy with his front view but ignoring the lack of material at the back. Out of sight, out of mind maybe. This caused me to laugh uncontrollably for a minute, but then suddenly to burst into tears because it was such a pathetic and unbelievable thing to witness.

That night Duncan and I raided the wardrobe to get clothes for the old man. Although they would obviously be too big for him, they would certainly be better than what he was wearing right now. The next day he turned up at the office as instructed and was feeling much better. He left happily with some money to see him through until his next visit, and clutching his bag of treasure provided by Duncan. The poverty in this country was heart-breaking, but the people were amazing, showing no self-pity and they were always extremely grateful for any help that they received. Was it any wonder that we loved this country and the people so much?

23

SEÑOR FELIZ

There was a clothing factory next door to our premises in San Marcos. They manufactured beautiful clothes for children, and quite often Adriana and I would visit to check out and buy the merchandise. In particular the beautiful baby dresses that they produced. The owner was a very serious man, who never smiled and because of this we named him Señor Feliz (Mr Happy). His employees confirmed that he was a harsh boss and frequently fired staff for trivialities. With high unemployment in the country, he had no problem finding replacements, and this resulted in a very fearful workforce. He was also notorious for trying to save money and cost cutting wherever he could. We never knew his real name but Señor Feliz also had a problem with his dentures not fitting correctly, (probably because he didn't want to pay for new ones), and struggled to keep them in place while talking. This of course was hilarious for all three of us in the office, but made it difficult for Adriana to keep her composure in order to converse with him (which she had to do because of the language barrier). One day Señor Feliz invited us to join him and his family for a weekend at his house in the mountains. Thankfully we couldn't make it due to a prior engagement but he kindly insisted that we go at a later date. Adriana, of course, thought this was comical as he didn't speak English and we didn't speak Spanish. So how could we communicate? Also, what about the loose dentures problem. There certainly wouldn't be many laughs with Señor Feliz's miserable face, but his dentures would maybe prove to be entertaining. We hoped that he would forget about the invitation as it would likely be too stressful for us. A few weeks later Señor Feliz came into the office looking more unhappy than ever. He explained to Adriana that he had received a bill from the power company for eleven hundred dollars. This was for a repair that was made in his property. However, he explained to Adriana (speaking slowly to retain his dentures) that he expected us to pay half of the cost.

When Adriana relayed this to me, I found it unbelievable, and asked her to question him about this. He reminded her that we rented half the building and he rented the other half. I agreed but since we had no problem with the power in our building and we had separate premises and accounts with the power company, I couldn't see his logic. I told Adriana in no uncertain terms that there was no chance of us giving him one red cent towards the cost. I'm sure Señor Feliz got the message from my facial expressions and demeanor, because he stormed out of the office, bill in hand, and still shouting. It was a miracle that he kept his dentures in place because he was so angry! After he left Adriana told me through fits of laughter that looking on the bright side, we would not have to endure the weekend in the mountains with him, as the invitation had now been revoked!

24

FUNERAL

Having been resident in El Salvador for nearly two years now, we were fortunate enough to be invited by friends to a number of different events – baptisms, weddings, baby showers, graduations, and various parties, including one at the American Embassy when we accompanied Nancy Hoffman and she introduced us to the American Ambassador and his wife, who were extremely friendly and mentioned they had Scottish ancestors. However, it was inevitable at some point that we would probably have to attend a funeral, and indeed when a lady from our church died, we were sad but honoured to attend this.

It was a beautiful day and in a lovely cemetery, that we were familiar with as we used to pass it every day on our way to our office in San Marcos. A huge congregation attended, but thankfully we arrived in good time to the graveside, where canopies were set up to provide shade and a choir was singing softly the hymn Amazing Grace. It was an impressive sight and very emotional, with the audience sitting reverently listening, heads bowed. Some were crying and some were praying but all, I'm sure, were recalling memories of our dear friend. We took our seats, but suddenly after a few minutes, loud music interrupted the beautiful scene. It was Duncan's mobile ringtone, playing El Jarabe Tapatio (The Mexican Hat Dance). This is a loud, jolly, fast tune and must be the most inappropriate music ever to be heard at a funeral. I expected the mariachis to appear any minute! Even worse, Duncan answered the call and proceeded to have a conversation (very loudly), with a customer interested in buying sewing machines. I could not believe his insensitivity, and gave him a kick to remind him where he was. I always knew Duncan's philosophy was that the business had priority, but even over a burial? Once again we were centre of attention, with people straining to see where the noise was coming from. The mood was ruined, and the choir's beautiful singing faltered, (probably because they lost interest in their performance due to the interruption), and the focus of the congregation's attention was now on Duncan's conversation also, rather than the music. Needless to say we left at the earliest opportunity, an embarrassing experience for me, but for Duncan a welcome opportunity to get another sale!

25

ELEANOR

Our daughter, Eleanor came to visit us with her partner, Matthew. I remember her telling us that it was an interesting journey. When she checked in for the flight at Houston, she was asked the reason for her trip to El Salvador. When she said it was to visit her parents, the agent enquired if we were missionaries there, which confused her. She was reprimanded on the plane for painting her nails; meanwhile, one passenger had boarded with a canoe, with no repercussions, or any second looks. Many of the passengers were returning home to El Salvador, so it was normal practice for them to take a chicken takeaway on board. Pollo Campero was extremely popular and, as far as Salvadorans were concerned - essential for the journey. Needless to say the aroma of fried chicken on the plane was overpowering but, strangely enough, Eleanor's nail polish seemed to cause more offence. What a weird flight!

On arrival to San Salvador airport, customs had to be cleared with, of course, the traffic lights system. Matthew got the green light and therefore had no problem. However, Eleanor (being her mother's daughter) got the red light, much to the agent's disgust, and was instructed to move on in spite of this, with no inspection being performed. It was probably the same agent that we met on our arrival, who showed the same lack of interest or urgency!

Lots of children crowded round us when we tried to exit the airport, following us and begging for food and money. Eleanor and Matthew found this to be quite intimidating as they had never experienced this in such huge numbers before. Also, they found it embarrassing when people were curious and stared. Duncan and I on the other hand were used to this and it didn't concern us. We tried to explain it's because we looked so different, and that's the reason for the interest.

The volcano close to our house disturbed them too, even though it was inactive, and Duncan and I hardly noticed it. Food also was a problem, with Eleanor being vegetarian. There wasn't much variety of vegetarian food as we know it, although we did our best to search for it.

Adriana took them out with some of her friends. This made them feel more comfortable, with both parties (Salvadoran and British) being interested in hearing about their respective countries and what life was like in particular for people of their ages. Overall, Eleanor and Matthew were shocked at the huge differences between El Salvador and the UK. Maybe this was because they had never experienced a country like El Salvador before and had expected it to be similar to Spain or Greece. Which it certainly was not. They stayed with us for a week and then we all travelled to attend Sarah-Jayne and Colin's wedding in Cuba, meeting up with family there and having a fantastic time in the beautiful resort of Varadero. It was wonderful, but we were there for only a few days, and were sad when it was time to leave and return to the reality of El Salvador and the business. The guests, including Eleanor and Matthew, returned to the UK, leaving Sarah-Jayne and Colin to enjoy their honeymoon in Cuba.

26

ALEJANDRO FERNANDEZ

Duncan had a gym membership at the Radisson Hotel, and would attend a few times a week. One Saturday morning, arriving there at his usual time, he was surprised to see a number of security guards positioned both inside and outside the building. When he drew nearer, a guard tried to stop him from entering. However, Duncan brushed past him, showing his membership card, and continued to the gym. There was only one other occupant there and he approached Duncan, offering his handshake and introducing himself as Alejandro Fernandez. Duncan shook his hand

and replied, "Duncan Young." Their respective exercise programmes continued, with some polite pleasantries being exchanged.

On leaving the hotel, Duncan noticed the same security guards still in place. He was shocked, however, at how their attitude towards him had changed, as their manner was now very respectful and polite.

On Monday morning, arriving at the office, Adriana was engrossed in reading the newspaper La Prensa Grafica. She explained that she was a fan of the famous Mexican singer who had appeared in concert there a couple of days ago. Unfortunately, she hadn't managed to get tickets, and was disappointed at having missed his performance. Glancing at the pictures on the front page, Duncan commented casually, "That's the guy that I met in the gym on Saturday, at the Radisson Hotel, and his name is Alejandro." Adriana nearly fell off her chair in shock. She demanded to know exactly what was said and all the details of their meeting. She couldn't believe that Duncan had managed, despite all the security, to share a private gym session and also have a conversation with the world famous singer Alejandro Fernandez. Even more unbelievable was that Duncan was completely unimpressed and also unaware of the singer's identity: when the majority of the Salvadoran population would have given their right arm to meet him!

27

EASTER PLAY

Duncan was becoming more and more involved in the social aspects of the Union Church. He volunteered when invited to help with the security of the annual summer fete – although I advised him it would be safer for everybody, if he didn't accept the gun that was offered! Also, the gardening project was progressing well, as was the treehouse, being built for the pastor's children and also any children attending the church. It was when Pastor Jeff announced that they were having the annual Easter play, I was not surprised when Duncan volunteered and was cast as a Roman centurion positioned at the bottom of the cross at the crucifixion. Although he only had one line to say, Duncan took the role seriously, with many hours of practice taking place. I of course offered advice to the best of my ability, but I was no Meryl Streep.

The dialogue was "This man truly was the son of God." Duncan proceeded to rehearse by putting emphasis on the various words in the sentence to establish the best way to deliver and therefore gain the impact that he desired. This MAN truly was the son of God, or this man TRULY was the son of God, or this man truly WAS the son of God, or This man truly was the SON of God, and lastly (my favourite), This man truly was the son of GOD. It was agreed that the last option was the best and I was happy when it was settled. Then foolishly I mentioned that John Wayne had this role in the movie (The Greatest Story Ever Told). Duncan then had the idea to deliver the line in an American accent similar to John Wayne's, and proceeded to do an impersonation. Fortunately I managed to persuade him away from this and to perhaps just proceed in his own accent. Thinking it would be preferable to increase the accent and his speech volume, Duncan managed to make the line incomprehensible even to me, so that idea was quickly dropped.

Eventually, after lots of practice, it was perfect, and Duncan eagerly awaited the date of the performance. At last it was the day of the play. The church was packed, and Nancy Hoffman and I sat nervously, giggling in the audience, hoping that Duncan would remember his line, but at the same time, wouldn't trip over his elaborate costume, or even the cross. As Duncan's line was the very last one in the play, we had a long time to suffer before his performance. Eventually it was Duncan's cue, and he delivered his line perfectly, (maybe some would say in the style of Liam Neeson). Nancy and I applauded and cheered furiously, and were convinced that Duncan had outperformed even John Wayne. We were so proud and agreed an Oscar would have been well deserved for Duncan! Meanwhile, he was announced this would be his first and last attempt in the acting profession as he had decided to return to his first love of entertainment, which was performing at the karaoke!

28

SHOPPING

Adriana and I had our favourite shopping places. We usually visited them while on our way to or from the business errands that we did for Duncan. The Hilasal Towel Factory, for example, was a great shopping venue, with lots of beautiful towels at good prices. The beer factory La Constancia was another of our haunts; there we were able to buy glasses and tee-shirts printed with slogans of Pilsiner, which was Duncan's favourite beer. At the side of the road there were always people selling fruits and also local food, which we would buy and take back to the office for lunch. The pupusas, and pastelitos, being our particular favourites. (Salvadoran cheese tortillas and deep fried crispy turnovers filled with meat or vegetables)

I also enjoyed the Mercado National de Artesanias, which sold traditional crafts of clothing and wooden items made in El Salvador. I bought brightly painted tables, stools, trays and vases to take home as gifts for friends and family. The craftsmanship and value for money was exceptional and everybody loved them, because they were so colourful.

We were also frequent visitors to the local market in San Marcos and, as usual, were the centre of attention with the locals, curious about us. One particular morning Adriana was shocked to read in the local newspaper, *La Prensa Grafica*, that somebody had been killed in a shooting there after a disagreement over the price of goods. Since we had been there a few days before, we felt really scared and Adriana told me that we shouldn't be going there as it was too dangerous. I remarked to her that we would leave it for a few days and then continue our visits, as I really enjoyed our shopping trips there. Adriana, however, knew better and told me that our visits there were terminated forever, because she didn't want me to be the next victim, while negotiating a bargain. She knew me so well!

29

FRIENDS

Our circle of friends had grown considerably. We met lots of people from different backgrounds and nationalities through the Union Church. One of these was Terry Youngblood from Texas, who worked in the American Embassy with Nancy Hoffman. We used to meet with Terry at Nancy's house most Tuesday evenings. Nancy was the perfect hostess and a wonderful cook and everything she served was delicious. Her chicken curry was a particular favourite of ours. Usually it was just the four of us there and we had fabulous times, with no shortage of laughs or conversation. Terry had a dry sense of humour and always had interesting and hilarious stories to tell.

One Sunday morning in church, a friend of ours who worked at the British School mentioned that a new teacher from Scotland had arrived. He offered to pass on our details as we were anxious to meet him. Tom Campbell contacted us a few days later and we arranged to pick him up at the school in Santa Tecla. He was extremely friendly and easy to talk to, and relieved to meet us, as he knew nobody in El Salvador. This was the start of our friendship and we took him to all our favourite restaurants, including Nancy's Bar.

Duncan and Tom had a lot in common, with football being their favourite subject. The first time that Tom stayed in our apartment, and was looking at Duncan's book collection, he suddenly shouted excitedly "You've got my book!" Sure enough, there it was: *Jock Stein, The Celtic Years* by Tom Campbell. He was delighted and insisted on signing it for Duncan.

Tom was an intellectual and had recently retired from teaching English literature at a Scottish university. He had signed up for a six-month contract at the Academia Britanica Cuscatleca, to relieve his boredom. On his first day of teaching there, the Head Teacher mentioned that he hoped Tom would last longer than the former teacher, who only stayed in the school for forty-five minutes. Thirty of which he had spent in the bathroom, shaking in terror. He was petrified and booked a flight home as soon as possible, unable to deal with the culture differences between the UK and El Salvador. Tom had no such issues and felt comfortable both at the school and wherever we went. He was friendly, and popular with everyone. We were sad to see him leave at the end of his contract, but will never forget the happy times spent with him.

Another friend of ours was Wende, an American lady who came from a famous family, and was introduced to us by Nancy Farlow, at her bar. Wende regaled us of her life growing up in Los Angeles, and of her parents socialising with The Kennedy's, Frank Sinatra, and Judy Garland, to mention just a few. She remembered all these people from her childhood, describing them as her parents' friends and neighbours. She told us that one time her dad invited her to accompany him to play tennis with a friend, but she chose not to go, preferring to watch television instead. She admitted to us that she did regret it when she discovered the friend was Charlie Chaplin.

One evening a few months after we met her, we were discussing movies, when she casually mentioned that her aunt was an actress. We asked if she had appeared in any well-known movies, she replied that although she was quite well known and had been nominated several times for an Oscar, but had never won. It transpired, after further questioning, that the aunt was Glenn Close! There was never a dull moment with Wende around, telling her unbelievable and shocking stories of the lives of the rich and famous in Beverly Hills.

At the end of 2003 and just before we left to return home for Christmas, we decided to host a party for our friends. We decided to have it at Mackie's Bar, in Escalon. We had known Mackie for some time and visited his bar often. Having travelled extensively after leaving his home country of the Philippines, he had lived in Los Angeles previously, but finally settled in El Salvador. He also kept us entertained with stories of his adventures. We invited our friends to the party and Mackie organised Chinese food to be served. We also invited Nancy Liévano's mother (Cony), who arrived and entered by herself, not in the least intimidated by the fact that she knew nobody there, apart from us. Since Adriana's parents were also there, we decided that they would be the ideal company for Cony, together with Nancy Hoffman, who also spoke Spanish fluently, and I knew that Cony would be comfortable with all of them.

The food was delicious and everyone had a lovely time. Cony enjoyed the food also, and when I enquired if she would like anything else, she replied that she would like another Cuba Libre (her favourite rum and coke cocktail). Soon after, Cony wanted to leave so Adriana and I took her home. On the way she was chatting and giggling like a schoolgirl and I remember thinking that if her family saw her this way, we would be in big trouble. When we arrived at the house everything was quiet and in darkness, with the household asleep. We rang the bell and Miguel answered, followed by Ana Maria. Cony was still in the same happy mood and loudly wished us good night, laughing as she entered the house. I think we can safely say that the party was a big success with everyone, including Cony, although I'm not sure that she would be permitted to socialise with us again!

30

THE END OF AN ERA

The year 2004 was to be our final year in El Salvador. It transpired that many of the American clothing manufacturers who moved to El Salvador had excess machinery, and so there was no market demand for our products. Also, the machine attachments that we sold did not interest them either, as they preferred to take advantage of the cheap labour available, instead of investing in items which saved time and therefore manufacturing costs. On top of all that, China was starting to open up, with even cheaper manufacturing costs and so businesses moved there in huge numbers. The UK office was continually asking us for more sales, and it was soon evident that El Salvador could not provide the massive revenue that they expected.

We decided in May 2004 to cease trading and informed the UK partners of our decision. They surprised us, however, by instructing us to leave the office open and requested us to move to China and open up a business there. I did not have to think twice and declined the offer, but Duncan readily accepted. My reasoning was that my parents were becoming frail and I was now needed at home to be close to them. I understood that Duncan needed to have a job, so he would move to China and we would try to see each other as often as possible. Adriana agreed to continue working for us to see how things would progress.

At the end of October 2004 we left, Duncan to go to China and myself to Scotland. We decided to go via Los Angeles, as Duncan required a Chinese visa which he could collect from a company in Pasadena, and it would also give us a chance to say goodbye to Nancy Liévano and all the family. Our friends at the Union Church organised a leaving party for us and presented us with a beautiful inscribed Salvadoran plate.

Leaving El Salvador and all our friends – Nancy Hoffman and Terry, Adriana, Cony, Ana Maria,

Miguel, Mackie, and all our church friends – was a traumatic time for us However, we knew it was time to move on and start a new chapter in our lives.

A few months after leaving El Salvador, Adriana called to say that she had accepted a position with another company, and therefore Sahl Americas had to be closed. Duncan returned and together they prepared the machines for their return to the UK office. This was the end of our business connection with El Salvador.

31

THE CHINA SYNDROME

At the end of October 2004, I arrived home to Scotland and Duncan arrived to a new adventure in Guangzhou, China. I suffered with a guilty conscience of not being there with him, but I knew that my place was at home as my mother and father needed my help. After a few weeks of job hunting, I secured a full-time position working in Aviva selling motor, home and travel insurance, in their call centre in Perth. It was a huge building, on four levels, with sixteen hundred people employed there. I had never worked in a place that size before. However, I soon settled in to the routine and it was a relief to be busy. Our house, which had been rented by a family from Kuwait with five children, had been left in a terrible condition. Windows and doors were damaged, carpets were filthy and furniture broken. It was a massive task to renovate, and I knew it would take some time before it would be comfortable again for us.

In the meantime, Duncan had settled into a four-bedroom house, in the Clifford Estate, Panyu, in Southern China. He employed a secretary, called Annie, to assist him, and it was her task to source companies and make appointments. Much the same job as Adriana had in El Salvador, but it was soon evident that she was not as interested or as capable as our dear friend. The one good thing about the Clifford Estate was the many former British colleagues of Duncan's living there. They were happy to have Duncan in Panyu and also to recommend him to their new employers. They knew from previous experience that he was good at solving sewing production problems (this being his speciality), and therefore would be helpful to them.

Another reason for opening the business in China was that there had been an assurance from a Chinese company and their British manager of their eagerness to deal with Sahl, which was Duncan's UK employers. Duncan soon found that travelling to visit customers was a problem and usually required a full day to make the round trip. Since Annie did not drive and Duncan could not legally drive, it was decided to hire transport. On the first day, the driver appeared late. Duncan had yet to be introduced, but was inspired to call him Long-Lie, after he explained he had overslept, and had a lie-in (which we would call a long lie). This was to be his name from then on and the name everyone knew him by – even the Chinese!

A few months after Duncan had settled in, I booked a flight to China for my first visit. Since there was no airport at Guangzhou at this time, Duncan met me in Hong Kong, where we stayed overnight. Next day we took the ferry to Nansha port in southern China. I was shocked at the huge number of people on the ferry and was sure it would capsize. I was also fascinated by the way they all munched food continuously, and didn't make conversation with each other, preferring to concentrate on the important task of eating. The food did not smell appetising and I hoped this would not be the norm everywhere in China. Duncan told me there were beautiful hotels in the Clifford Estate and assured me that I would be happy with the menus there. Since Duncan's choice of food was varied, and he would eat almost anything, I was not convinced this would be the case.

On arrival at the port, the first thing I noticed was the grey and dull appearance of the sky. Even though it was midday, and quite warm, there was no sun. Buildings, windows and cars, in fact almost everything outside, were all covered in thick grime, making a depressing picture. It wasn't long before I had to reach for my asthma inhaler as the heavy atmosphere was making me breathless. This was to be my experience every time I visited China.

Duncan's house was beautiful and very roomy. Annie worked in an office there, so there was no need to rent business premises. The estate was huge, with schools, hotels, restaurants and even a hospital. There was a small shopping centre which I visited often and bought lovely stoned bracelets to take home, as gifts. The local children took to following me on my shopping trips, (being curious of my appearance). Giggling excitedly when I appeared, and waiting patiently outside each shop, and finally following me home again, at a safe distance. Making me feel like the Pied Piper!

The supermarket, though, was not pleasant. Live chickens in cages were up for sale and the smell of the meat especially was very pungent. Duncan and

I had no idea what food to buy, with everything being written in Chinese, so had to be guided by the pictures on the packets and tins. One evening he took me to The Manhattan Restaurant in the Clifford Hotel. It was an impressive place and the restaurant was very grand. Duncan advised me to check out the buffet, thinking it would be better to see what was available, rather than trying to decipher the menu. However, the way the food was presented at the buffet was not appealing and did not stimulate my appetite at all. The duck on the barbecue had not been carved and lay there in an awkward pose, complete with head. No way would I sample that! The mashed potatoes had little worm-type creatures mixed in. That was another no-no! By this time my appetite had understandably disappeared and I returned to the table with only ice cream. To be honest, even that I wasn't sure about, and kept examining it for unwelcome visitors. I visited China a few times, and my impression of it did not change with experience.

Duncan, however, settled in really quickly and was kept busy with the business. He didn't mind the food and was happy to try most dishes. His British colleagues would gather at the Owl Bar in the Clifford Estate at the weekends and he was happy to join them for the company. The business was doing well, with lots of enquiries about the different types of machinery and parts that Sahl International offered. We tried to see each other every twelve weeks, with either me visiting China or Duncan visiting home. It wasn't easy, but we had no choice, as there was no market for industrial sewing machine sales in Scotland.

On one of my visits to China, Duncan was excited to show me the motor cycle he had bought. He said it would be easier for us to get around the estate to visit the shops, restaurants and bars. I agreed. The only problem was that I could not get on it! Being so short, I couldn't get my leg high enough to climb on and so Duncan reluctantly had to lift me, remarking that I really had to lose some weight! I think Duncan had the impression that we would resemble the Easy Rider movie, which was popular in the sixties, but it was far from that! Especially as the crash helmets didn't fit right, and we must have made a comical picture, with mine being too big and Duncan's too small. It only occurred to us later that I was wearing his and he was wearing mine! However, there was no stopping us running around the estate, complete with the wrong helmets, to the amusement of the curious Chinese people. I couldn't understand what was so funny until Duncan explained it was unusual for European people like us to use this form of transport in China, as normally chauffeur-driven vehicles would be hired and passengers would sit in comfort.

After a few days visiting local places, Duncan suggested that we venture outside the estate and visit a sports town in the hills. He had heard that there were genuine branded clothes and shoes at cheap prices to be had there, and so a visit was planned with a few friends accompanying us. After driving a short distance, we came to a river bank, where a man with a tiny boat operated a ferry scheme. We all piled on, complete with motor cycles, and the journey lasted all of two minutes and cost pennies. It was hilarious and bizarre. Later we stopped for drinks at an outside cafe, but declined the owner's offer to cook for us. The sports village was packed with all the items you could imagine and we were laden with treasure. It didn't occur to me as to how I would get this back to Panyu, but I refused to leave anything behind, and so the tiny package compartment on the bike was tightly packed. We tied items everywhere we could on the bike, leaving hardly any room for us. On leaving the village the local children ran alongside us to wave us off, and at one point even overtook us! What a great day with lots of happy memories – not to mention the great bargains we got!

On another occasion, Duncan arranged for us to meet some friends at a bar. When I enquired about the location he assured me that it wasn't far, and was called The Cohiba. He also mentioned, to my horror, that it was a topless bar. He was puzzled when I objected going to such a place, and assured me that it was impressive, and he had gone there a lot, which made me even angrier. We arrived at the place and it was a huge restaurant. In spite of my searching (and to my relief), I could see no topless ladies. We ordered dinner and it arrived. However, each item was served on a different plate. Fries were separate from the steak and the vegetables. Also, I was given four glasses when I ordered vodka and coke – one with vodka, one with coke, one with ice and another empty. This was so that I could mix it myself as the bar staff had no clue. It was comical. The table was covered with random plates of food and drinks, causing confusion about who had ordered what. When it grew dark, suddenly, loud music started. It was the theme from the Space Odyssey 2001 movie. To combine with this dramatic music, the roof slid slowly back to reveal a beautiful evening sky with sparkling stars. This was the topless bar! To be fair, I had to agree that it was impressive!

Another time we made the trip to Guangzhou, with a few friends. The main reason for the trip was to visit the Irish bar and get some appetising food. There were great clothes shops there too and it was fabulous buying presents to take home, for family and friends. After a couple of hours shopping we arrived to Paddy Fields, and had a wonderful steak pie dinner, followed by a few drinks. When it was time to leave, we ordered two taxis and piled into one of them and stored our precious purchases in the boot of the other one, leaving a friend in charge of it, in the other taxi. It was a long trip back, so we were soon fast asleep. The driver had to wake us up when we arrived back in Panyu. Somebody suggested a nightcap at the Owl Bar. We eagerly awaited our friend arriving with our purchases from the other taxi. We couldn't believe it when he arrived – empty handed. He had let the taxi go with our precious cargo. All our hard work and searching for great bargains had been for nothing. Duncan asked me if I knew the name of the taxi company but of course I didn't. The only thing that I remembered was that the driver was Chinese!

After Duncan had been living in China for sixteen months, the company decided that he should move to a smaller house to reduce living costs. He managed to lease a three-bedroom apartment in a different location in the Clifford Estate, with one bedroom to be used as an office. The apartment was large and spacious with a beautiful garden complete with fish in a pond! With a substantial reduction in the rent it seemed perfect. The secretary, Annie had left by this time and was replaced by a lovely girl called Yhen. I arranged a flight to coincide with the move in order to be there to help Duncan. It all went well, although it took a few days to get everything organised, and the business was soon able to re-commence again. That weekend we met with Duncan's friends and he told them about the house move. They were surprised, but even more so when they discovered the new apartment was on the ground floor. Apparently, everybody avoided these apartments due to the huge number of suicides in China, and this was why the rent was so cheap. It was common for people to go onto the roof and jump off, landing in the garden of the ground-floor apartment. Of course this was news to us, but it was too late to do anything about it, and fortunately nothing like that ever happened.

One night in the Clifford Hotel, we discovered a karaoke taking place. When we entered the venue, of course everybody as usual turned to look at us.

This was common, as people were curious about anybody who was not Chinese. We were shown to our table and given the song list for our selections. Duncan suggested a duet but I hastily declined. He soon had selected a number of his favourite songs for his performance. As he took his position on stage, you would have thought Frank Sinatra himself was about to perform. People were shouting encouragement in Chinese, and whistling and clapping. I was extremely nervous, but Duncan was unaffected by all this attention. He took his position on the stool and casually picked up the mike. The music started, but when the words appeared on the screen in Chinese, he was stunned. Quickly an adjustment was made and the words in English appeared. Duncan gave a great performance, to the delight of the audience He was given a noisy round of applause and an encore was requested. Duncan introduced the next song, saying, "For my next number I'm going to sing, 'My Way'." More songs were performed, and after the last one, people climbed onto the stage to have their pictures taken with him. What an unbelievable evening and a reception that even Frank Sinatra would have been proud of!

Duncan called me one day at home to explain that he had experienced an incident with the motor cycle. Although he was not legal to drive outside the complex, one day he decided he would take a chance and venture outside. Unfortunately he was stopped by the police who demanded to see his driver's licence. He began frantically searching through his wallet for the non-existent licence, wondering in panic how he would get out of this one. Then suddenly he found the fake Frank Sinatra identification card that I had bought for him in Los Angeles. It came complete with photo of Frank Sinatra and all his details: Date of birth, hair and eye colour, address, and occupation (which was noted as swooner). Thinking it was worth a try, Duncan confidently handed over the card. The police officer examined it closely, taking time to compare Duncan with the picture and eventually handed it back with a grunt, saying, "You go." He must have thought this was a genuine American driver's licence, and was happy with the Frank Sinatra photo and the comparison with Duncan. We couldn't wait to relate the story at the Owl Bar. When he did, all his friends requested similar cards from me on my next visit to Los Angeles. I had orders for i.d. cards of Brad Pitt, Johnny Depp, Clint Eastwood and Jean-Claude Van Damme, to name a few! As promised I bought the cards on my next visit and soon all these famous celebrities were confidently riding around China on little motorcycles!

After Duncan had been in China for approximately four years, the company decided to transfer him to Bangkok, Thailand, because business was expanding and he was needed there. Duncan was happy to comply and so a new adventure was about to begin!

32

TREASURES OF THAILAND

Duncan began working at the Sahl International office in Bangkok, Thailand. He had visited the office many times before, so was familiar with the staff and their names. He remembers how, when he was first introduced, they laughed when they heard his name. Weird, especially coming from ladies called, Oye, Gift, Boom and Pooh. He was able to stay in his boss's apartment. It was lovely, with a great view of the river, where brightly lit tourist boats sailed up and down and could be viewed from the apartment balcony in the evenings.

Duncan adapted to his new life once again and was soon kept busy, both in the office and visiting customers. We had the same routine as before, visiting each other every twelve weeks. I was anxious to see Bangkok, after hearing that the shopping was amazing, and indeed it was! The market at Patpong sold everything – clothes, shoes, handbags, sporting goods and jewellery. They opened in the evenings until midnight, and the stallholders loved to haggle over prices. There were restaurants on either side of the stalls, so we usually shopped first and ate later.

On one occasion we heard that there was to be an Elvis impersonator performing. We found the venue, took our seats and eagerly awaited his performance. The Thai Elvis was hilarious, about half the height of Elvis and a quarter of the size, and looked about twelve years old. He ran onto the stage in a sparkly white jumpsuit, demonstrating all his Elvis moves. It was interesting because, being Thai and having a very thick accent, the English pronunciation of the words were difficult but hilarious to decipher. We'll never forget him singing 'The Wunda of You', 'Jailhouse Lock' and 'Suspicio Minds'! All in all it was a great night, and it was only after we got home that we discovered we had left all our purchases in the bar:

too fascinated with Elvis to remember them. We returned the next night to Patpong to buy everything again. We received a lovely welcome from the puzzled but happy stallholders, who of course had remembered us from the night before, and were delighted to sell us everything again. That night we visited the restaurant once more, but waited until Elvis had left the building (not wanting to be hypnotised by his performance a second time!).

Bangkok was certainly an interesting place. Lines of traffic everywhere, with the noise and pollution horrendous. Motorcycle taxis were popular, as they were able to weave in and out of the traffic jams easily. I remember one evening, sitting at a table outside a bar, being startled when an elephant suddenly appeared beside us. His keeper asked if I would like to feed it for a small fee. I had no idea how to do this but he gave me the maize and quickly but gently the elephant took it from my hand. Unbelievable that such an animal had to endure all the hazards of such a busy city.

On another visit, we took a short flight to Chang Mai, which is about four hundred miles north of Bangkok. We went to visit Eleanor's English friends, Liz and Graham, who lived there permanently. We booked a luxurious hotel in the centre of the city, which was amazingly grand but very cheap. Liz and Graham took us to some interesting places, including the Maesa Elephant Sanctuary. The camp seemed to be well maintained and the elephants well cared for. They were fabulous, playing football and then painting pictures of trees, which were very clear. We recognised that this was not their natural setting, but compared to the elephants being led around the busy streets of Bangkok, at least they were in a safe environment. We had an amazing time there, and left in awe of the elephants and their talents. Chang Mai was a miniature version of Bangkok, with its numerous restaurants and great shopping. Liz and Graham were wonderful hosts and made our trip extremely interesting and enjoyable.

On my return to Scotland and while wearing one of my new Thai blouses, my workmates were impressed by the quality and asked if I could bring some home for them and their families. After thinking about it I decided to ask Duncan to enquire about prices for buying men's polo shirts in bulk (thinking it would be easier to manage the men's sizing rather than ladies) from the street market in Bangkok. I calculated that we could make enough money to possibly pay for our flights, which would be a great help financially. Duncan called me from the market, and gave me the stallholder's price. In my opinion, it was excessive, given the quantity we were purchasing, and so I asked Duncan to let me talk to the man. I persuaded him to give us a better price, since we were buying a large quantity, and hopefully this would be a repeat order every few months, giving him a guaranteed order. He understood and agreed, realising the potential business we could offer him. So it was arranged and Duncan returned home every twelve weeks with the polo shirts, which were readily snapped up by my colleagues. Word spread around the office and soon I had a line of people at my desk, collecting and paying for tee-shirts and ordering more for the next delivery. A friend in the office commented that my tee-shirts were so popular that it was starting to look like the company uniform! I remember one of our weekly sales meeting when my boss, as usual, asked about our sales figures. My colleague Tom Shek, eagerly informed the meeting that I had sixteen sales that day. I had to confess, though, to the manager, that this was polo shirts and not insurance policies. I was lucky to keep my job!

After approximately four years in Thailand, Duncan decided it was time to retire. He was exhausted with the travelling and living away from home. Also, we now had two grandchildren, Alfie and Amber, and Duncan was missing them and all the family. He was eager to spend more time at home. So it was decided, he was coming home, but I secretly wondered how long for, as it would be a massive change for him to be back in Scotland permanently. Only time would tell if it was the right decision!

33

FOR A FEW DOLLARS MORE

After being home for only a few months, Duncan was offered employment by a company in Mexico. He would be self-employed and on a rolling contract term. Finding it difficult to adjust to retirement, he quickly accepted the new position. The company was in Ixtlahuaca, approximately twenty-five miles from Toluca. It was a small town, with a few restaurants, bars and shops. I imagined it to be similar to the towns in the Clint Eastwood spaghetti westerns, with Mexicans wearing sombreros, propped up outside bars while dozing in the midday sun.

Duncan stayed in a hotel in the town and once again settled in easily to working life abroad. I decided not to visit him there, because there would be very little for me to do, no tourist attractions to visit and Duncan would be busy with work. So we had to be content with his visits home. The company also had contracts with companies in India and Duncan was asked to visit there to look at various manufacturing problems. One evening, while there, he invited some colleagues to join him at his hotel. After dinner it was suggested that they retire to the rooftop bar and swimming pool for drinks. It was beautiful, situated in the centre of Bollywood (the location of the Indian movie making industry), and provided stunning views of the city.

On entering, Duncan noticed how busy the bar was, with a large group of noisy people ordering drinks close by. Suddenly a waiter approached Duncan and asked him if he would kindly agree to join the group at their table, as they were excited to meet him, and also that Missy requested a photograph with him. Much to the amusement of his friends, he reluctantly agreed, and proceeded to meet, shake hands and have pictures taken with a number of them (including Missy). Puzzled, he re-joined his friends, only to be informed that

Missy was a famous Bollywood star, and she thought that he was the Irish actor Liam Neeson! It must have been the similarities in height, colouring and his Scottish accent that was enough to convince her. It was hilarious, but Duncan was happy to comply and gratefully accepted the complimentary drinks that Missy provided for his party.

He was to visit India a few times, but it was not a country that he enjoyed. The poverty and culture differences made life difficult. After completing his contracts and returning to Mexico, he moved to work for a company in Jordan. The owner of the company was anxious to modernise the factory and its production processes, but the managers were not, preferring instead to use the cheap labour that the country provided. This led to confrontation and awkwardness between Duncan and staff and after six months, ultimately resulted with his resignation. This was enough to make him realise that times were changing and the hassle of working in a foreign country had lost its appeal. It was his final contract abroad and since then he has been content to remain in Scotland, enjoying his retirement!

34

THE FLAG

Jessica (Nancy Liévano's daughter), was a great fan of the soccer star David Beckham who played for L.A. Galaxy. She had met him before and had pictures taken with him at a Meet the Players Day, organised for season ticket holders by L.A. Galaxy. Together with her cousin Robert Rosales, they attended all the home games. On one of my visits to Los Angeles, Jessica mentioned that she was anxious to get the shirt that David Beckham threw into the crowd at the end of each game. She thought that if she had something to attract his attention, it would give her a better chance.

Her seat was behind the goal, in the first row of the stadium, with a little wall in front. I suggested an England flag to drape over the wall, might get his attention, but since England flags were displayed there already, that idea was dropped. I then mentioned the Union Jack, it being the flag of Great Britain and Jessica liked that idea, never having seen one in the stadium. When I got home, I scoured the internet for one. I was shocked when it arrived as it was much bigger than I had imagined, but sent it off to Burbank anyway. Jessica was delighted and couldn't wait to hang the flag on the wall in front of her seat.

Disappointingly, though, nothing happened and she never managed to get his shirt. That was until the day that David Beckham played his final game for the club, and L.A. Galaxy won the MLS cup. It was a big day for the team and also a fitting end to Beckham's career there, resulting in fabulous celebrations on the field, with press photographers and lots of excitement from the crowd. Jessica and Robert were enjoying the celebrations, when suddenly a young man approached them. He introduced himself as David Beckham's personal assistant, and asked if Mr Beckham could borrow her Union Jack to have some photographs taken with it? Jessica was delighted to help, but insisted that the flag be returned to her afterwards, and he readily agreed. The celebrations continued and everyone watched as Beckham and his family had pictures taken, covered with the flag, by the world's press. In the meantime Nancy and the family were watching the game on television, unaware that the flag featured was Jessica's. They were really upset, thinking that Jessica would be devastated. Frank, Nancy's son, commented to Nancy, "Who on earth would own such a huge flag anyway?" and added that it made Jessica's flag look inadequate. How wrong could they be! The phone rang: it was an excited Geri Rosales, informing them that Robert had called to say that it was indeed Jessica's flag being used.

After the celebrations ended and the crowd started to disperse, Jessica remained, waiting for her flag to be returned. After some time, she made her way to the dressing rooms in search of somebody to help her. A security officer appeared and instructed her to leave, saying that he knew nothing about a flag. However, Jessica stood her ground and insisted that she was going nowhere until her precious flag was returned to her, because that was the deal with David Beckham's assistant. The security guard reluctantly went to investigate and, after some time, returned with the flag, which was soaked with beer and champagne, and also – as Jessica remarked later – with David Beckham's DNA! She therefore didn't care about its condition, because it was unique and given the choice would prefer it to just another soccer jersey.

The next day, pictures appeared in numerous magazines and tv programmes, showing the Beckham family with Jessica's flag. She still has the flag, kept in a special case, and also the magazines featuring the photographs have been carefully stored. Who would have believed that a flag costing five pounds bought from the internet would have such a glamorous history? Approximately six months later, while in a hospital waiting room with my father, I picked up a Hello magazine and included was the picture of the Beckham family with the famous flag. I showed it to my dad, who was aware of the story and he gleefully related it to a young man sitting next to him, offering him the evidence in the magazine. However, the man was most unimpressed, and did not believe a word of the story, saying how did my dad know that this was the same flag? It could be any flag? My eighty-year-old father was furious and threatened to take him outside and beat him up. I had to hastily intervene and calm him down, explaining that, you couldn't blame the stranger for being sceptical, because it was a rather fantastic story. Nevertheless, we knew it was true, and one that we all (and especially Jessica) will never forget!

35

BARS

Looking back, it does seem that we had been in the habit of frequenting a number of bars in various different countries. In El Salvador, one of our favourites was La Herradura, and this is where we could be found every Friday night after work. It was a great bar, with friendly staff who had our drinks served and waiting for us by the time we parked and walked in the door. They served delicious pizzas too, but most of all the atmosphere was relaxed and the staff welcoming. The Zona Rosa had a number of bars too that we visited; usually La Hola Beto's would be our choice for

Sunday lunch, after church, with Duncan enjoying the ceviche (seafood marinated in citrus juices), in particular. Another evening, after visiting the British Club in Escalon, we came upon an interesting but noisy bar called No Way José. It was a karaoke bar and there was no shortage of volunteer singers to belt out hits at maximum volume. After spending an hour or so there, it was time for us to leave, unable to suffer any more of the loud music.

The next evening, in our Spanish class, Nancy Liévano complained of feeling really tired, and explained it was because of the noise coming from a karaoke bar across from her house in Escalon. Warning bells started to ring. She said that the singing was so loud and excruciatingly bad that it disrupted the family's sleep on a regular basis. Duncan and I started to laugh and she couldn't believe it when we confessed to having been there the night before. We had no idea that Nancy lived in that area, and in spite of us denying responsibility for the awful singing, I'm sure that she didn't believe us. However, we never returned to that bar, preferring somewhere quieter to visit.

Of course Nancy Farlow's Bar would be Saturday night's spot for us, with dinner and drinks and catching up with our friends, Wende and Tito, among others. One evening while driving home from work, we were delayed by a huge traffic jam. As we crawled along the road in the darkness, Duncan spotted a brightly lit sign advertising a bar called Los Ranchos. Thinking it might be a good idea to have a drink while we waited for the line of traffic to disperse, we made our way inside. It was empty, but soon after the cabaret started, with only us in the audience. It comprised of two short men playing guitars and one large lady performing songs in Spanish. I was delighted with their performance, being familiar with the songs, which had been included in the repertoire of my favourite singer, Nana Mouskouri for many years. The group being delighted with my appreciation of their music, eagerly offered to perform my requests – 'Volver Volver', 'La Paloma Blanca', 'Besame Mucho', 'La Golondrina', to name but a few – while standing a few inches away from our table, and therefore demanding our full attention. It was hilarious! Duncan, however, was not as impressed. The money in his wallet was reducing rapidly, as I had instructed him to tip them after every song. Eventually it was time to leave, and thankfully the traffic had gone. It was one of the first bars we visited in El Salvador and I can honestly say one of the most enjoyable, but maybe not the cheapest.

In China we visited the Owl Bar and also Paddy Fields for the steak and Guinness pie, and of course the Cohiba Bar (with retractable roof) for its delicious steaks, and the Clifford Hotel (not for food, but for drinks). In Thailand we visited a variety of bars which provided karaoke and good food.

In Los Angeles, we went to Izalco for traditional Salvadoran beer and delicious pupusas, and to Musso and Franks in Hollywood Blvd for lemon drop cocktails (and also to hear the stories of famous customers, related to us by the staff). This was the first restaurant constructed in Hollywood and the favourite place of The Rat Pack, Marilyn Monroe, and numerous famous actors. Duncan insisted on having his picture taken in Mr Sinatra's favourite booth there. We were shocked when, on arriving home after the holiday, we found his picture of the Rat Pack lying smashed on our kitchen floor. Obviously Old Blue Eyes was unhappy with Duncan's intrusion! Jameson's Bar was good for roast beef and fish and chips. Lala's in Studio City served wonderful dishes: it was introduced to us by Geri and Roberto Rosales. The Granville and The Olive Garden in Burbank, which we visited often, provided delicious food. The Snug, an Irish bar, was one of the friendliest bars we visited, often with Robert and Eddie Rosales, and which we now regard as our local, while we're visiting Burbank. One night Frank Sol (Nancy Liévano's son), took us to Dimples Karaoke Bar with his friend Trinity Courier and we spent a hilarious few hours there listening while great songs were being "performed," by various customers.

One of the most interesting bars that we visited in Los Angeles was close to our hotel. Tinhorn Flats Saloon was recommended to us by Eleanor, who spent an interesting afternoon there, hearing stories from out of work actors about their movie-making participations. Another interesting experience was when we visited Candilejas Bar, which reminded me of an old wild west saloon. It was noisy, to say the least, and packed, and as usual everyone stared when we entered. There were no empty seats and so we stood at the bar to order the drinks. We were surprised when the barmaid explained that they didn't sell liquor but only beer. Another surprise came when we asked for a glass and were told that they were all in use and so we had to wait for somebody to leave to have their glass. The toilets were a joy to visit as the barmaid provided the key on request, together with the toilet paper, with instructions that both had to be returned to her. By the time I came back from the toilet (and had returned the key and toilet paper), Duncan was happily playing pool with a group of men, and was reluctant to leave them. I stood nervously at the bar, anxious for somebody to leave so that I could have both their seat and their glass! Eventually we left and resisted the temptation to visit again!

All in all we have had lots of fantastic times in those bars, and many more, too numerous to mention. Maybe we were lucky, but I can honestly say that we never had a frightening or dangerous experience anywhere. Apart from some bars that we have visited in Scotland!

36

A FLIGHT TO REMEMBER

After we left El Salvador, we continued to visit Nancy Liévano and family in Los Angeles. We would arrange trips, wherever Duncan was based, by going or returning via Los Angeles. On one occasion in February, when Duncan and I were heading to visit Nancy, we experienced a long delay due to heavy snow, at New York while waiting for our connecting flight to Los Angeles. After being there for approximately four hours, we were advised that we had been upgraded and given fresh boarding cards. I took my seat in the middle of three, with Duncan sitting in front.

Soon the lady in the window seat started a conversation about her trip and how she was visiting her son who was a movie producer in Hollywood. She was looking forward to going onto the set and meeting the stars of the movie. I was impressed, and I remember thinking how exciting it would be to meet somebody famous. In the aisle seat a young blonde lady asked me to pass her shades, which were in the seat pocket in front of me. This broke the ice and a conversation started. When I mentioned that I was going to Burbank to visit friends, she commented that it was very close to her home in Beverly Hills. The conversation continued, with her enquiring where I was from, and when I asked if she had ever been to Scotland, she mentioned that she had visited London countless times but had never been to Scotland. The stewards in the meantime were serving her very promptly and courteously and I noted that she was prepared for the flight when she produced her own pillow. After chatting for some time, I had a nap and woke up to find a little chihuahua in her seat, while she was searching her luggage in the overhead bin. I commented to her that I nearly had a heart attack, as I never expected to see a dog on the flight. She sat down, taking the dog on her lap, and explained that he went everywhere with her, and his name was Peter Pan. He had been asleep in his dog carrier under the seat in front and this was why I had never noticed him before. It was only when she added that she had a total of seventeen dogs, that the penny dropped and I suddenly thought that she might be famous. All this time we were only about twelve inches apart and I hadn't recognised her! It was only when I said, "Oh no, don't tell me that you are famous!"

She giggled and whispered, "I'm Paris Hilton!"

Shocked, I said rather loudly, "No way!"

She laughed and put her finger to her lips, indicating to be quiet, not wanting to attract attention. After that I felt really shy, but she still chatted, while I petted Peter Pan, who seemed very placid and was obviously a seasoned flyer. In the meantime, I was shaking! I explained to her that I had watched a documentary of her recently with Fearne Cotton, the English television presenter, and was impressed when she allowed Fearne to try on some of her clothes and even gifted her a dress, because it suited her so well. She laughed, saying that Fearne was a sweetheart. When I mentioned that Eleanor was a fan of hers, she readily gave me her autograph to pass on and even included paw prints from Peter Pan!

Soon it was time to land and Paris started packing her belongings and gently put Peter Pan in his cute carrier. It was shaped like a car, complete with ornamental headlights. When I admired it, she replied that it only cost nineteen dollars. Miss Hilton was then allowed to disembark first, while the rest of us waited in our seats. As she left, she said goodbye, that it was a pleasure to have met me and she hoped that I had a good time with my friends in Burbank! I couldn't wait to tell Nancy and the family of this experience, and how nice Paris Hilton was to me. It certainly set my holiday off to a great start and reminded me never to believe all the negative stories about celebrities in the media.

37

GOOD TIMES IN
LOS ANGELES

We have had many fantastic times in Los Angeles, and took the opportunity to visit lots of different entertainment venues. Duncan, being a football fan, always enjoyed his visits to see LA Galaxy play. He was also fortunate to go to the Holly-wood Bowl with Sarah-Jayne, Colin and Roberto Rosales to see Tony Bennett, a favourite singer of his, in concert. It was on this same visit that we discovered that Engelbert Humperdink would be appearing in concert at the Starlight Bowl in

Burbank, which is a miniature version of the Hollywood Bowl and was situated close to our hotel. We managed to get tickets and were delighted to visit this beautiful open air venue, on a lovely warm evening. People were arriving with picnic hampers containing mountains of food, presumably to see them through the next two hours. We were shocked at the quantity of food being brought in and it dawned on us that we were seriously unprepared for this event, as the only supply rations we possessed were six beers and a bottle of wine! However, we had a great time and Engelbert proved to be an excellent entertainer and still possessed a wonderful voice. A fabulous evening, and one that we'll never forget.

You can imagine, therefore, how excited we were on another visit to Los Angeles when we learned that Engelbert was scheduled to perform at the Saban Theatre, in Beverly Hills. We eagerly bought tickets for ourselves and Roberto and also Catriona, (Duncan's sister), who was visiting with us at the time. The bar was packed before the performance began and Roberto pointed out the singer Pat Boone, waiting to enter the theatre. Since we hadn't managed to buy four seats together, Catriona and I took the two seats in the upper tier and Duncan and Roberto took the other two seats in the stalls. Engelbert appeared and the concert began. It was apparent that it was to the same high standard as the previous concert we attended in the Starlight Bowl. At one point Engelbert introduced a few celebrity friends in the audience and included Pat Boone. Meanwhile I was becoming quite uncomfortable, as I desperately needed to use the bathroom.

Hoping the interval would be soon, I postponed my visit as long as I could. However, when I could wait no longer, I mentioned to Catriona that I was going to the bathroom. I nervously made my way in the darkness to the exit, trying to find my feet and feel my way without tripping. However, surprisingly, there were no signs in the passageway to guide me to the bathrooms, so I proceeded to go down a large flight of stairs, still sign searching as I went. I then came to another flight of stairs going upwards, and had no option but to proceed. Suddenly, the voice of Engelbert was very loud and I then could see him singing on the stage through the curtain. I was in the wings of the stage! I hastily removed myself from the side of the stage and retraced my steps. I could not believe that I nearly shared a stage with Engelbert while looking for the bathroom, and no security in place to stop me! Eventually, I found the bathroom and then made my way back to my seat. On the way home I related my experience to my companions. Duncan was horrified, and said that he would have disowned me if I had indeed appeared on the stage, wandering around searching for the bathroom. We all laughed at this, but I have to admit it did remind me of a Mr Bean sketch! Even thinking about that experience now brings me out in a cold sweat!

During another of my visits to Los Angeles, I bought four tickets to see *The Sound of Music*, which was in the Walt Disney Concert Hall. Since we only needed three tickets for Nancy, Geri and myself, the extra ticket, was requested by Nancy for a friend. We were all excited on the evening of the show, as this was a particular favourite of ours, and eagerly made our way to pick up Nancy's friend. I have to say I was rather shocked when the "friend," turned out to be a nun! She was a sister of the Cabrini Mission of the Sacred Heart of Jesus, which is a Roman Catholic female religious order, and was founded in 1880. Sister Regina proved to be a highly entertaining companion, relating hilarious stories on the journey of her cat Moses, and various other subjects, including her Cabrini sisters.

The show was amazing and Sister Regina questioned me at the interval, eager to get my opinion of the Reverend Mother. Feeling unqualified to express my views, since my experience of convents and indeed Revered Mothers' were limited, I enquired about her thoughts. She readily answered, and so with no hesitation, I agreed with her that the Reverend Mother actress was convincing and outstanding. On our journey home we were once again entertained by Sister Regina with her recollections and memories. I remember recounting this experience to Eleanor, and she commented, "Only you, Mother, would be likely to attend *The Sound of Music* with a nun!"

38

MEMORIES OF ALLAN GRAY

My dad (Allan Gray), was delighted each time we visited Nancy Liévano and family in Los Angeles, as he was a big fan of American cigars and appreciated the duty free whisky. Each time, he gave us our instructions as to what to bring back. I remember the first time that I brought him "Scotch Whisky" from there. It was called, The Clan MacGregor and was in a one-and-three-quarter litre plastic flagon. I warned him that this was double the strength of whisky distilled in Scotland and therefore he had to be careful with the measures, as eighty percent proof whisky could be lethal. Laughing, he nodded his head and I knew he would take no notice of my advice.

The next day he called me asking exactly where I had bought the whisky, as the previous night he had invited his friend Jim to sample a few. He said that everything had been going great, with each recalling happy memories of their recent holiday in Canada, and their many adventures there. Suddenly an argument started, resulting in my dad challenging Jim to fight. However, neither of them could remember what caused the argument, so they agreed to disagree and have another whisky to celebrate their friendship. I was shocked and told my dad in no uncertain terms that I would never bring that whisky again, as it was so powerful. However, he disagreed and insisted that they both had a fantastic night and looked forward to my next trip to Los Angeles, and to receiving further supplies of The Clan MacGregor!

On another occasion, my dad visited me at home, as I was due to leave for Los Angeles the next day. He asked if he could do anything to help me get organised for my trip. I suggested that he tidy the back garden and I would do the front. He disappeared carrying a gadget called the grass burner, which was a metal rod fitted with a gas cylinder which produced a small flame. This was useful for burning weeds between the concrete slabs. Just a few minutes later I heard my dad calling excitedly, "Heather, Heather, come quick and see this!" Thinking he had found money or treasure, I rushed to find him. I can honestly say that I nearly had a heart attack when I saw what had happened. He had managed to set alight to the hedges at the back of the garden, by mistakenly going too close to the small branches underneath with the grass burner. Smoke was billowing and flames starting to spread and my dad shouted, "Get some water in a bucket!"

I ran around in panic, looking around for my non-existent bucket, and shouted back, "I don't have a bucket!"

My dad retorted, "What do you mean? Everybody has a bucket!"

I replied, "I don't."

He then stopped, deep in thought. "Now where did I see cheap buckets? There were lots, all piled up and different colours too. Some orange, some black, some red. Was it Tesco or Asda or—"

At this point I interrupted him as the flames were now changing their direction and were heading towards the house. I immediately called the Fire Brigade in a panic, as I was sure further disaster was imminent. Thankfully they arrived a few minutes later and to my relief soon had the fire under control. I thanked them profusely and the fireman said, "As I said to your husband these grass burners can be really dangerous and have been responsible for a lot of fires."

I wasted no time in correcting him. "He is my dad, not my husband!"

Meanwhile my dad was laughing his head off, delighted at being mistaken for my husband. All that was left of the hedges, were blackened twigs, and although my dad insisted that they would grow again, they never did and eventually had to be removed. As far as the grass burner was concerned, it was binned the same day. However, I can report that I am now the proud owner of a bucket, which I bought at my dad's insistence!

39

THE SALVADORAN
CONNECTION

Since Duncan's retirement, we have been content to limit our travels to visiting our friends in Los Angeles. Our adventures, however, have never stopped and often we find ourselves in comical situations. I remember in particular one occasion when I travelled alone to visit Nancy Liévano. The Super Shuttle driver that picked me up at the airport that day, was not in a good mood, and since I was the only passenger, the silence on the long journey was quite awkward. To relieve the tension, I nervously asked him where he was from (having noticed his accent when he gruffly assisted me with my luggage). When he replied reluctantly that he was from El Salvador, I was immediately relieved and excitedly told him that I used to live there. However, glancing at me in his mirror he did not seem convinced; understandably, he probably found this hard to believe. He began questioning me in order to test my knowledge of El Salvador. He asked why we were there, where we lived, could I name any restaurants or bars that we had been to? Of course I was able to answer all his questions in detail (especially about the bars). This changed his attitude and he began to be interested, laughing when I related some funny stories of our experiences there and obviously excited to talk about his homeland. He was a proud Salvadoran and was delighted that we had enjoyed our four years in his country. However, I had one more piece of evidence of our Salvadoran residency that I was sure he would approve of. When I produced my mobile phone and played him the ringtone, he almost drove off the road in shock. It was the national anthem of El Salvador, which is one of my favourite tunes and an obvious choice for my ringtone. By the time I arrived at Nancy's house, José had invited me to meet his wife and to dinner at his house. He said that he couldn't wait to tell her about the crazy Scottish lady that he met and to relay all my stories of El Salvador to her. As he drove off, waving happily, Nancy asked how I knew him. I told her, only as the bus driver, and described how we chatted on our way here. She laughed. "That Salvadoran connection again follows you wherever you go!"

We had many similar experiences in Los Angeles. Once, in The Snug, Duncan had a conversation with a young Salvadoran couple, who stayed with us all evening and were extremely sociable, inviting us to their house to meet the family, an invitation which unfortunately we couldn't accept, due to prior commitments. However, these chance meetings always bring back happy memories of our time in El Salvador and reconfirm our opinion of how wonderful the people are, by the welcome that they give, and with our mutual respect and interest in each other's countries, proving that the connection between us is stronger than ever.

We haven't managed a return visit to El Salvador but hopefully, one day, we will. It would be wonderful to reconnect with some of our friends again, and also to visit the Union Church, which occupied a significant part in our lives there. Maybe we would even visit our old office in San

Marcos, and it would be exciting to see the structural and social changes in the country. Although a visit to our old gang member friends would probably be better avoided!

Printed in Great Britain
by Amazon